CONTENTS

Maps | [Map Number | Map Name | Page Number | Section Number]

Contact: All inquiries and correspondence should be sent to Indian Chief Publishing House, P.O. Box 1814, Davis, CA 95617, or *info@indianchief.net*.

Book data: The Complete Maui, Molokai and Lanai Guidebook, 3rd edition, ISBN 0-916841-77-4.

Contributors to this book: B. Sangwan, David J. Russ, Kiran Savage-Sangwan.

Printed in the U.S.A.

HOW TO USE THIS GUIDEBOOK

This guidebook is divided into five chapters: Overview, History, and three *Exploring the Island* chapters, one each for Maui, Molokai and Lanai. Each of the *Exploring* chapters is subdivided into sections, areas, segments, and points of interest (see below).

Section: **MAUI**
Area: **Lahaina**
Segment: *Exploring Front Street*
Point of Interest: ***Banyan Tree***

What the Icons and Numbers Mean:

This guidebook is sectioned, and entries in it cross-referenced, to enable you to quickly and easily find what you are looking for, a lot like links on web pages on the Internet. And that is where the icons and numbers come in—as a link.

 Icon: This ubiquitous icon is a prod for you to reference a corresponding map for orientation or, if you are already looking at a map in the book, to reference a corresponding section or area where you will find more information.

Numbers are of three different kinds:

1 **Section Reference:** At the start of each section, such as West Maui or Road to Hana, a small island map with a rectangle defining the area covered in the section appears, together with a number that corresponds to the number-coded section on the larger island map at the start of the chapter. This is designed to enable you to reference the section on the map for an overview and orientation.

Entries Between Rules: Also, where sections are lengthier, a list of areas covered in the section appears between parallel rules directly beneath the section heading. This is designed to enable you to quickly find the area relevant to your interest.

 Area Reference: At the start of most areas, such as Lahaina or Kihei, a black number in a gray box appears. This corresponds to the number-coded area map relevant to the text. This is designed to orient you with the area.

3 **Point of Interest Reference:** Alongside several entries in the book, a white number in a gray box appears in the side margin. This corresponds to the point of interest located on the referenced area map (described above, in Area Reference). This will enable you to find the relevant points of interest quickly and easily.

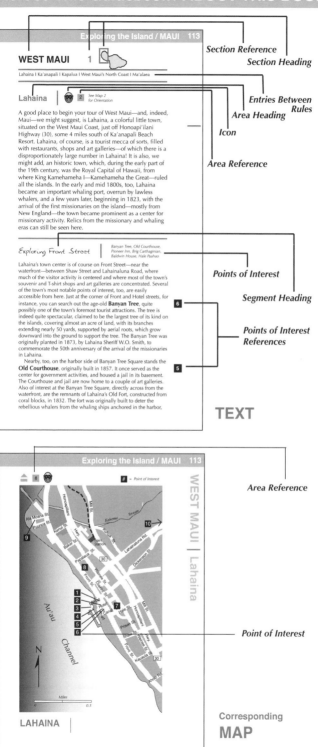

Section Reference

Section Heading

Exploring the Island / MAUI 113

WEST MAUI 1

Lahaina I Ka'anapali I Kapalua I West Maui's North Coast I Ma'alaea

Entries Between Rules

Area Heading

Lahaina 2 See Map 2 for Orientation

Icon

A good place to begin your tour of West Maui—and, indeed, Maui—we might suggest, is Lahaina, a colorful little town, situated on the West Maui Coast, just off Honoapi'ilani Highway (30), some 4 miles south of Ka'anapali Beach Resort. Lahaina, of course, is a tourist mecca of sorts, filled with restaurants, shops and art galleries—of which there is a disproportionately large number in Lahaina! It is also, we might add, an historic town, which, during the early part of the 19th century, was the Royal Capital of Hawaii, from where King Kamehameha I—Kamehameha the Great—ruled all the islands. In the early and mid 1800s, too, Lahaina became an important whaling port, overrun by lawless whalers, and a few years later, beginning in 1823, with the arrival of the first missionaries on the island—the town became prominent as a center for missionary activity. Relics from the missionary and whaling eras can still be seen here.

Area Reference

Exploring Front Street | Banyan Tree, Old Courthouse, Pioneer Inn, Brig Carthaginian, Baldwin House, Hale Paahao

Lahaina's town center is of course on Front Street—near the waterfront—between Shaw Street and Lahainaluna Road, where much of the visitor activity is centered and where most of the town's souvenir and T-shirt shops and art galleries are concentrated. Several of the town's most notable points of interest, too, are easily accessible from here. Just at the corner of Front and Hotel streets, for instance, you can search out the age-old **Banyan Tree**, quite possibly one of the town's foremost tourist attractions. The tree is indeed quite spectacular, claimed to be the largest tree of its kind on the islands, covering almost an acre of land, with its branches extending nearly 50 yards, supported by aerial roots, which grow downward into the ground to support the tree. The Banyan Tree was originally planted in 1873, by Lahaina Sheriff W.O. Smith, to commemorate the 50th anniversary of the arrival of the missionaries in Lahaina.

Nearby, too, on the harbor side of Banyan Tree Square stands the **Old Courthouse**, originally built in 1857. It once served as the center for government activities, and housed a jail in its basement. The Courthouse and jail are now home to a couple of art galleries. Also of interest at the Banyan Tree Square, directly across from the waterfront, are the remnants of Lahaina's Old Fort, constructed from coral blocks, in 1832. The fort was originally built to deter the rebellious whalers from the whaling ships anchored in the harbor,

Points of Interest

Segment Heading

Points of Interest References

6

5

TEXT

Exploring the Island / MAUI 113

8

■ = Point of Interest

WEST MAUI | Lahaina

Area Reference

Point of Interest

LAHAINA

Corresponding **MAP**

OVERVIEW

The Islands | Getting There | Getting Around | Tourist Information

The Islands

The Hawaiian islands lie approximately 2,400 miles southwest of the west coast of mainland USA, smack in the middle of the Pacific Ocean. The archipelago includes well over a hundred atolls, reefs, shoals and tiny islands spread out over some 1,600 miles of ocean, but there are only eight major islands in the chain: Oahu, Hawaii (the Big Island), Kauai, Ni'ihau, Maui, Molokai, Lanai and Kaho'olawe.

In this book, we cover Maui, Molokai and Lanai, which—together with the uninhabited island of Kaho'olawe that was a U.S. Naval bombing range until quite recently—make up Maui County.

Maui  See Map 1 for Orientation

Maui, alternately known as the "Valley Isle" and the "Magic Island," is the second largest of the Hawaiian islands, encompassing 729 square miles. It comprises two distinct, volcanic land masses, West Maui and East Maui, joined together by a low, central valley, or isthmus. The island lies approximately 35 miles northwest of the Big Island of Hawaii, with Molokai and Lanai to its north and west, respectively, each some 9 miles distant. The island of Oahu lies 75 miles to the northwest of Maui.

Maui has a population of more than 85,000, and is one of the most popular destinations in Hawaii, drawing more than 2.5 million visitors annually. It has no fewer than 13,000 hotel rooms and rental condominium accommodations, more than 200 restaurants, and offers a wealth of recreational opportunities, including swimming, snorkeling, scuba diving, windsurfing, sailing, whale-watching, hiking, biking, horseback riding, golfing, and beachcombing. It also boasts, on the average, 320 days of glorious sunshine a year.

Molokai   11 See Map 11 for Orientation

Molokai, dubbed the "Friendly Isle," is the fifth largest island in the Hawaiian archipelago, 38 miles long and 10 miles wide. Like Maui, it is also comprised of two volcanic land masses, East Molokai and West Molokai, joined together by a dry plain that makes up Central Molokai. The island lies 8½ miles northwest of Maui, 9 miles north of Lanai, and 25 miles southeast of Oahu.

Molokai is the least developed of the Hawaiian islands, with no major resorts, and no building on the island taller than a palm tree. But it does offer hotel and condominium accommodations and abundant outdoor recreational opportunities, including swimming, snorkeling, sailing, fishing, hiking, horseback riding and golfing. Did we mention kite flying?

Lanai

 14 *See Map 14 for Orientation*

Lanai, once known as the "Pineapple Isle" for its prolific pineapple crop, but now successfully transformed into the "Private Isle," is the sixth largest Hawaiian island, 18 miles long and 13 miles wide, encompassing some 141 square miles. Unlike Maui and Molokai, Lanai comprises a single, volcanic land mass, with its highest point more or less at the center of the island. Lanai is situated 9 miles south of Molokai and 8½ miles west of Maui.

The island, which is owned entirely by a single corporation, is fairly rugged, but does offer luxury resort accommodations and fine dining, snorkeling, scuba diving, sailing, fishing, hiking, beach-combing, and golfing at world-class golf courses.

Getting There

Airports, Airlines and Ferries

The good thing about going to Maui is that you have the option of either flying there directly, non-stop, from mainland USA, or traveling through the busy hub at Honolulu International Airport on the island of Oahu, and from there on an inter-island flight to Maui. There are also inter-island flights between Honolulu, Oahu, and Molokai, and Honolulu and Lanai, as well as between Maui and Molokai, and Maui and Lanai. Additionally, inter-island ferries ply between Maui and Molokai, and Maui and Lanai.

Airports

Maui has three airports: at Kahului, which is the island's principal airport, and two smaller ones at Kapalua and Hana. Molokai's main airport is at Ho'olehua, in Central Molokai, with an airfield located on its Kalaupapa Peninsula. Lanai has just one airport, located 3 miles southwest of Lanai City.

Airport Contacts:

Kahului Airport, Kahului, Maui; (808) 872-3893

Kapalua Airport, Kapalua, Maui; (808) 872-3830

Hana Airport, Hana, Maui; (808) 248-8208
Molokai Airport, Ho'olehua, Molokai; (808) 567-6361
Lanai Airport, Lanai City, Lanai; (808) 565-6757

Traveling Direct to Maui

The following airlines fly direct to Maui from the continental U.S.:

Delta Airlines (800) 221-1212/www.delta.com
United Airlines (800) 864-8331/www.united.com
American Trans Air (800) 435-9282/225-2955/www.ata.com
U.S. Air (800) 428-4332/www.usairways.com

Traveling Via Honolulu

Domestic Airlines flying to Honolulu:

American Airlines (800) 433-7300/www.aa.com
America West Airlines (800) 235-9292/www.americawest.com
Delta Airlines (800) 221-1212/www.delta.com
Hawaiian Airlines (800) 882-8811/www.hawaiianair.com
Northwest Airlines (800) 225-2525/www.nwa.com
United Airlines (800) 864-8331/241-6522/www.united.com

International Airlines flying to Honolulu:

Air New Zealand (800) 262-1234/www.airnewzealand.com
Air Canada (888) 247-2262/www.aircanada.com
China Airlines (800) 227-5118/www.china-airlines.com
Japan Airlines (800) 525-3663/www.jal.co.jp/en
Korean Air (800) 438-5000/www.koreanair.com
Philippines Airlines (800) 435-9725/www.philippineairlines.com
Singapore Airlines (800) 742-3333/www.singaporeair.com

Inter-Island Flights

There are several airlines offering multiple flights daily between Honolulu and Maui, Honolulu and Molokai, and Maui and the islands of Molokai and Lanai. Typically, fares for travel between Honolulu and Maui range from $69-$149 one-way, to $138-$298 round trip. Multi-day, unlimited travel passes are also available.

Honolulu to Maui, Molokai and Lanai:

Aloha Airlines (808) 244-9071/(800) 367-5250/www.alohaairlines.com

Island Air (808) 877-5755/(800) 652-65417(800) 323-3345/
www.islandair.com

Hawaiian Airlines (808) 871-6132/(800) 367-5320/882-8811/
www.hawaiianair.com

Maui to Molokai and Lanai:

Aloha Airlines (800) 367-5250/www.alohaair.com

Hawaiian Airlines (800) 882-8811/(800) 367-5320/www.hawai-
ianair.com

Hawaii Air Taxi (808) 329-7157/(866) 799-8294/www.hawaiiair-
taxi.com

Island Air (800) 652-6541/www.islandair.com

Mokulele Flight Service (808) 326-7070/(866) 260-7070/www.
mokulele.com

Pacific Wings (888) 575-4546/www.radixx.cc/pacificwings/book-
ing/restst.asp

Paragon Air (866) 946-4744/www.paragon-air.com

Inter-Island Ferries

There are, in addition to inter-island flights, daily ferry services
available between Maui and the islands of Molokai and Lanai.
Ferry boats shuttle between Lahaina, West Maui, and Kaunakakai,
Molokai, and Manele Bay, Lanai. The fare for adults, from Maui to
Molokai, is around $40.00 one-way, and from Maui to Lanai, ap-
proximately $26.00 one-way.

Maui to Molokai Ferry:

Maui Princess, 658 Front St., Suite 101, Lahaina, (808) 661-
8397/(877) 500-6284/www.molokaiferry.com or www.mauiprin-
cess.com

Maui to Lanai Ferry:

Expeditions, Lahaina, (808) 661-3756/(800) 695-2624/www.
go-lanai.com

Getting Around | *Car Rentals, Taxis and Shuttles*

Taxis as well as airport and, in some cases, inter-resort shuttles are available on Maui. But the best, most convenient and possibly the least expensive way to get around the islands of Maui, Molokai and Lanai is in a rental car or SUV.

Car Rentals

Rental cars typically rent in the range of $18-$130 per day on Maui, $20-$100 on Molokai, and $50-$140 on Lanai. Weekly rates range from $150.00 to $320.00 on the average.

Car Rentals on Maui:

Alamo, Kahului Airport, (808) 871-6235/(800) 327-9633/*www. alamo.com*

Avis, Kahului Airport, (800) 831-8000/*www.avis.com*

Budget, Kahului Airport, (808) 871-8811/(800) 527-0700/*www. budget.com*

Dollar, Kahului Airport, (800) 800-4000/(800) 342-7398/(866) 434-2226/*www.dollar.com*

Hertz, Kahului Airport, (800) 654-3131/(800) 654-3011/*www. hertz.com*

National, Kahului Airport, (808) 871-8851/(800) 227-7368/ *www.nationalcar.com*

Thrifty, Kahului Airport, (800) 847-4389/*www.thrifty.com*

Kihei Rent-A-Car, Kihei, (808) 879-7257/(800) 251-5288/*www. kiheirentacar.com*

Adventures Rent-A-Jeep, 571 Haleakala Hwy., Kahului, (808) 877-6626/*www.mauijeeprentals.com*

Car Rentals on Molokai:

Budget, Ho'olehua, (808) 567-6877/(800) 527-0700/*www. budget.com*

Dollar, Ho'olehua, (800) 342-7398/(866) 434-2226/*www.dollar. com*

Island Kine Auto Rentals, Kaunakakai, (808) 553-5242/(866) 527-7368/*www.molokai-car-rental.com*

Molokai Outdoor Activities, Kaunakakai, (808) 553-4477/*www. molokai-outdoors.com*

Car Rentals on Lanai:

Dollar Rent A Car, 1036 Lanai Ave., Lanai City, (808) 565-7227/(800) 342-7398/*www.dollar.com*

Shuttles and Taxis

Airport shuttles operate between Kahului Airport on Maui and the premier resort and visitor areas. Taxis are also available from the airport to the island's population centers and resort areas. Fares, typically, range from $30-$45, and from the airport to Ka'anapali and Kapalua, $40-$75. On Molokai, It is approximately $20-$25 from the Molokai Airport in Ho'olehua to Kaunakakai. On Maui, complimentary shuttle services between Ka'anapali and Kapalua and Ka'anapali and the Wharf Shopping Center are also available.

Maui Shuttles:

Akina, (808) 879-2828/*www.akinatours.com*

Maui Tours and Transportation, (808) 283-0145/(877) 874-5561/*www.mttours.com*

Speedi Airport Shuttle, (808) 661-6667/(808) 875-8070/(877) 521-2085/*www.speedishuttle.com*

Maui Taxis:

Ali'i Cab, (808) 661-3688; *Sunshine Cabs,* (808) 879-2220; *Wailea Taxi,* (808) 874-5000; and *Yellow Cab of Maui,* (808) 877-7000.

Molokai Taxi and Shuttle:

Molokai Off-Road Tours & Taxi, (808) 553-3369.

Tourist Information

*Visitors Bureaus,
Department of Parka and Recreation,
Weather and Time*

Visitors Bureaus:

Hawaii Visitors and Convention Bureau (HVCB). Waikiki Business Plaza, 2270 Kalakaua Ave., Suite 801, Honolulu. HI 96815; (808) 923-1811/(800) 464-2924/*www.hvcb.org* or *www.gohawaii.com.* This is Hawaii's principal, one-stop source for visitor information, both for published materials and online information. The "gohawaii" web site has all the reference materials you could want, including listings for accommodations, restaurants, events, tours and recreation. The bureau also offers a free, cover-all publication in its visitor package, *The Islands of Hawaii: A Vacation Planner,* with a wealth of tourist information on places of interest on the islands, recreational opportunities and a wide selection of tours.

Maui Visitors Bureau. 1727 Wili Pa Loop, Wailuku, HI 96793; (808) 244-3530/(800) 525-6284/*www.visitmaui.com*; Open 8 a.m.-4 p.m., Mon.-Fri. Wealth of tourist information available, including directory of accommodations and restaurants and a calendar of events. Also maps, and Hawaii's premier, free tourist publication, *The Islands of Hawaii: A Vacation Planner*s. A useful web site for a calendar of events on Maui is *www.calendarmaui.com.*

Molokai Visitors Association. P.O. Box 960, Kaunakakai, HI 96748; (808) 553-3876/(800) 800-6367/*www.molokai-hawaii.com.* Also offers visitor information, for accommodations, restaurants, tours and events on Molokai. Open 8 a.m.-4.30 p.m., Mon.-Fri. Two other web sites for useful information for visitors to Molokai are *www.visitmolokai.com* and *www.molokaievents.com.*

Chambers of Commerce:

Maui Chamber of Commerce. 70 W. Ka'ahumanu Ave.. Kahului, HI 96793; (808) 871-7711/*www.mauichamber.com*; open 8.30-4.30, Mon.-Fri. Visitor information brochures, including lodging, restaurant and tour company listings.

Molokai Chamber of Commerce. P.O. Box 515, Kaunakakai, HI 96748 (located at the Molokai Center, Ste. 108, Molokai); (808) 553-3773/*www.molokaichamber.org.* Visitor information brochures, including lodging, restaurant and tour company listings.

Department of Parks and Recreation:

Maui County Department of Parks and Recreation, Maui Office. 1580C Ka'ahumanu Ave., Wailuku, HI 96793; (808) 270-7383/*www.co.maui.hi.us/departments/Parks.* Information and permits for camping in county park areas in Maui, Molokai and Lanai.

Molokai Office. P.O. Box 1055, Kaunakakai, HI 96748; (808) 553-3204.

Lanai Office. P.O. Box 793, Lanai City, HI 96763; (808) 565-6979.

Weather:

For current weather conditions and forecasts for Maui, call (808) 877-5111.

Time:

For current Hawaiian Time, call (808) 242-0212.

STORY OF MAUI | A Brief History

Maui began forming nearly 5 million years ago, when a series of eruptions on the ocean floor created two adjacent, shielded volcanoes. These, with the accumulation of molten lava over a period of time, finally emerged as Pu'u Kukui and Mount Haleakala, 5,788 feet and 10,023 feet above sea level, respectively, with a low, central isthmus joining the two land masses. Then, approximately a million years ago, Pu'u Kukui became extinct, and Mount Haleakala dormant. In the following years, rivers, streams, ocean waves and the wind sculpted and shaped the island, forming valleys, canyons, cliffs and mountains.

Legend, however, endures that it was Hawaiian demigod Maui who fished out the island of Maui and the other Hawaiian islands from the sea, when his fish-hook became caught at the bottom of the ocean. Demigod Maui, we are told, also forced the sun to slow its passage over Hawaii, when he lassoed the sun's rays from atop Mount Haleakala, "House of the Sun," in order that the islands may enjoy longer days of sunshine.

Maui's earliest inhabitants were the Marquesans, a Polynesian people who journeyed to Maui from the Marquesas and Society islands between 500 A.D. and 750 A.D., followed some years later, around 1000 A.D., by the Tahitians. The Marquesans, who journeyed to Hawaii in large outrigger canoes, navigating by the stars across several thousand miles of open ocean, introduced to Maui and the other Hawaiian islands the first domestic animals, plants and fruit; and the Tahitians, for their part, brought with them their religion and their gods and goddesses, notable among them Kane, the god of all living creatures; Ku, god of war; Pele, goddess of fire; Kaneloa, the god of the land of the departed spirits; and Lono, god of harvest and peace. The Tahitians also introduced to the islands the *kapu* system, a strict social order that affected all aspects of life and formed the core of ancient Hawaiian culture.

The first white man to sight Maui was Captain James Cook, a British explorer in search of a northwest passage from the Pacific Ocean to the Atlantic Ocean. He first sighted Maui in 1778, during his second expedition to the Pacific and the Hawaiian islands, but did not land on the island. In the ensuing years, others followed, notably French nobleman and navigator Compte de la Perouse, and Captain George Vancouver, another British explorer. La Perouse landed on Maui at La Perouse Bay, near the southern end of the island, in 1786, and became the first European to set foot on Maui. Vancouver arrived in 1792, landing at Kihei, on the southwest coast of the island, and returned in 1793, bringing with him live cattle and root vegetables, which he first introduced to Maui. These early Europeans, however, also brought with them to the Hawaiian islands the white man's disease. Hawaiians had little or no resistance to Western diseases, and over a period of some 100 years following Cook's first contact with the islands, nearly 80% of Hawaii's indigenous population was wiped out.

The mid and late 1700s also ushered in Hawaii's era of monarchy. Kamehameha I—also known as Kamehameha the Great—was born in the late 1750s, and by 1791 he had gained control of the island of Hawaii. In 1794, following the death of King Kahekili of Maui, he conquered Maui as well as the nearby islands of Lanai and Molokai. The following year, in 1795, in his bid to bring all the Hawaiian islands under his rule, Kamehameha also conquered Oahu; and a few years later, in 1810, he extended his dominion, through diplomacy, to include Kauai. Subsequently, Kamehameha the Great, the king of all the Hawaiian islands, established his capital in Lahaina, on Maui's west coast, and there he built his "Brick Palace," one of the first Western structures to be erected in the island. In 1843, however, the capital of the Hawaiian islands shifted from Lahaina to Honolulu, on the island of Oahu.

The year 1819 witnessed the arrival of the first American and British whalers in Maui, giving birth to the island's early whaling industry. Lahaina became an important whaling port, and for the next half century it remained one of the rowdiest, most boisterous towns in the islands, filled with whorehouses, saloons and gambling dens, overrun by lawless whalers. In 1846, at the height of the whaling activity, more than 400 whaling ships docked in the Lahaina Harbor, but by the early 1870s, with the decline of whaling, Lahaina's whaling era had drawn to a close.

In 1823 the first missionaries arrived in Maui, at Lahaina. Among the earliest and most notable were William Richards, Ephraim Spaulding and Dwight Baldwin. Over the years, the missionaries established missions, churches and schools, with much of the activity centered in Lahaina, where they built the Old Fort in 1832 to deter the rowdy whalers, and founded the Lahainaluna Seminary—notably the oldest educational institution west of the Rocky Mountains—a year earlier, in 1831. The seminary housed one of the first printing presses in the West, the Hale Pai, on which the very first Hawaiian-language newspaper was printed in 1834. The missionaries were also the first to develop the written Hawaiian language, comprising 12 alphabets—5 vowels and 7 consonants—and translate the Bible into Hawaiian. In 1824, Queen Ka'ahumanu, the favorite wife of Kamehameha I, became one of the earliest and most important converts to Christianity.

The early 1800s also brought to prominence David Malo, acknowledged as Hawaii's first scholar. Malo was one of the earliest graduates of Lahainaluna, who, wary of Hawaii's disappearing culture, wrote the definitive history of the Hawaiian people and their culture, *Hawaiian Antiquities,* in which he detailed the origins of the Hawaiian people and described life under the ancient *kapu* system, as well as Hawaiian culture and traditions. In 1847, Malo became a minister at the Kikolani Church, where he preached until his death in 1853.

The late 1800s witnessed the birth of Hawaii's sugar industry, followed in the 1920s by the pineapple industry. Large sugarcane and pineapple plantations were developed, mostly by descendants of the early missionaries. Businessmen Henry Baldwin and Samuel Alexander, for instance, founded Maui's sugar dynasty when they joined forces to form the Alexander & Baldwin Company, which remains to this day the largest private landholder as well as largest employer on Maui. Alexander & Baldwin also became charter members of Hawaii's Big Five—the islands' five largest corporations that controlled Hawaii's economy and politics for more than half a century.

The late 1800s and early 1900s also brought to the Hawaiian islands waves of immigrants—mostly Chinese, Japanese, Filipino, Portugese and other Europeans—drawn to Hawaii's growing sugar and pineapple industries. Over time, the number of these new immigrants turned Hawaii's indigenous population into a minority. On Maui, in fact, pure-blooded, native Hawaiians now comprise only 15% of the population, and on Lanai, just 10%.

In the late 1800s also, after the death of Kamehameha V, Hawaiian monarchy fell into disarray, and the custom of electing a king was established. At about this time, too, with the growth of Hawaii's sugar industry, American interests on the island increased. In 1892, upon the start of open rebellion, the *U.S.S. Boston* landed an armed force on the island of Oahu to protect American interests, and a year later, in 1893, a more or less bloodless revolution brought to power, at the head of a provisional government, Sanford B. Dole. The following year, Hawaii was declared a republic by the Hawaiian legislature, and on June 14, 1900, Hawaii was annexed, under the Organic Act, by the United States, and a territorial form of government established.

In 1902, Prince Jonah Kuhio Kalanianaole, born of royal parentage, and the last heir to the throne, became the first Hawaiian delegate elected to the U.S. Congress. Kuhio led the Hawaiian congressional delegation for the next two decades, and despite not having an official vote in the legislature—as Hawaii was only a territory of the United States at the time—he forged important legislation for the betterment of Hawaii and its people. Among his triumphs: the landmark Hawaiian Homesteads Act of 1910 and the Hawaiian Homes Commission Act of 1921, whereby public lands were made available to native Hawaiians for homesteading. He also obtained funding for such important projects as the Kahului Harbor, Maui's only deep-water port, and Pearl Harbor at Honolulu, and in 1919 and 1920, he introduced two successive bills for statehood for Hawaii in the U.S. Congress. In 1922, Kuhio died at the age of 50.

On August 21, 1959, Hawaii finally gained statehood, becoming the 50th state of the nation—the "Aloha State." That same year, the first commercial jet, a Boeing 707, landed in the islands, at Honolulu, greatly reducing travel time from the continental U.S. to Hawaii, to under 4½ hours. This, effectively, signalled the beginning of tourism in Hawaii.

In the following decade, Hawaii's tourist era began in earnest. On the island of Maui, in the 1960s, Ka'anapali Beach began to develop into a premier resort, beginning with the construction of the Royal Lahaina Hotel in December, 1962, and the Sheraton Maui in 1963. Also in the 1960s, the Lahaina Historical Foundation began an ambitious project to restore the historic whaling port of Lahaina—now a tourist mecca of sorts—to its former glory. In the 1970s, the Alexander & Baldwin Company developed the exclusive Kapalua Resort on Kapalua Bay in West Maui; and on the southwest coast of the island, the first luxury hotels and resorts at Wailea were constructed. In 1980, the Stouffer Group of Hotels acquired Hotel Hana and transformed it into a lavish beachfront hotel, and Chris Hemmeter, Hawaii's most famous developer, opened to the public the multimillion-dollar Hyatt Regency. In the 1980s, too, yet more resort hotels sprang up on the island's west and southwest coasts, including the Maui Marriott, Maui Prince Hotel and, the grandest of all, the $155-million Westin Maui.

In the mid-1970s also, Maui's business leaders began promoting their island as a separate tourist destination—apart from the other Hawaiian islands—and quickly developed it into one of Hawaii's foremost tourist meccas. Championship golf courses were developed at the resorts to lure world-class tournaments, a commuter airport was built at Kapalua in West Maui, and condominium complexes sprang up all along the west coast of the island—notably at Napili, Honokowai and Kihei—most with an eye to drawing the upscale visitor. The island now attracts more than 2.5 million visitors each year—second only to Oahu.

The latter years have also witnessed the creation and preservation of a series of state parks and sanctuaries. In 1969, for instance, the 44-square-mile Haleakala National Park, which was originally established in 1916, added to its acreage the ancient Kipahulu Valley; in 1971, Makena Beach State Park was created; in 1977, the Molokini Marine Reserve was established just off the coast of Maui, as a sanctuary for endangered seabirds; and in 1978 and 1979, respectively, the Waianapanapa and Iao Valley state parks were set aside for public use. Also in 1979, the Ahihi-Kinau Natural Area Reserve, encompassing 2,045 acres, including an 807-acre undersea ecological reserve, was established on the site of the most recent lava flow on the island, which occurred in 1790.

Maui is now poised as a premier destination resort, with an abundance of excellent hotel and condominium accommodations and restaurants and other visitor facilities, and a wealth of recreational opportunities, including surfing, windsurfing, snorkeling, scuba diving, sailing, golf, tennis, helicopter touring, and more.

MAUI | The Valley Isle

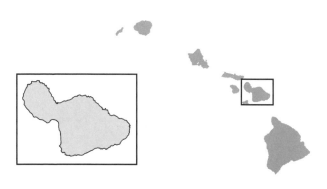

Maui | Exploring the Island

Maui is "no ka oi!" (the best). That is what visitors to the island and locals will tell you. After all, it has some of Hawaii's best beaches, best resorts, best golf courses, and best weather, with an average of 320 days of sunshine a year.

Maui encompasses approximately 729 square miles, and is made up of two volcanic land masses, West Maui and East Maui, joined by a low, central valley, or isthmus. West Maui, the smaller and drier of the two, owes its existence to the extinct Pu'u Kukui, elevation, 5,788 feet, and boasts the island's premier resorts, Ka'anapali and Kapalua, and the historic, tourist-alluring town of Lahaina. East Maui, larger and more varied, is home to Maui's principal towns, Kahului and Wailuku, and towering Mount Haleakala, elevation 10,023 feet (the highest point on Maui), the mid to lower reaches of which make up Upcountry, the fertile cradle of Maui's agriculture. East Maui also includes the southwest coast of the island, where Kihei, Wailea and Makena spill over onto sandy, sun-drenched beaches, and the rain-soaked, lush countryside along the Road to Hana.

For the purposes of exploring the island, we have divided Maui into five distinct sections determined by logical geographic groupings and patterns of travel:

1 **West Maui**, which includes Lahaina, Ka'anapali, Kapalua, West Maui's North Coast and Ma'alaea;

2 **Southwest Coast**, which takes in Kihei, Wailea and Makena;

3 **Central Maui**, made up of the twin communities of Kahului and Wailuku;

4 **Upcountry**, which includes Makawao, Kula and the Haleakala National Park;

5 **Road to Hana**, which sets out from Paia, taking in the east and southeast coasts of the island, and ends at Hana.

[The numbers in the sidebar correspond to those in the number coded map of the island.]

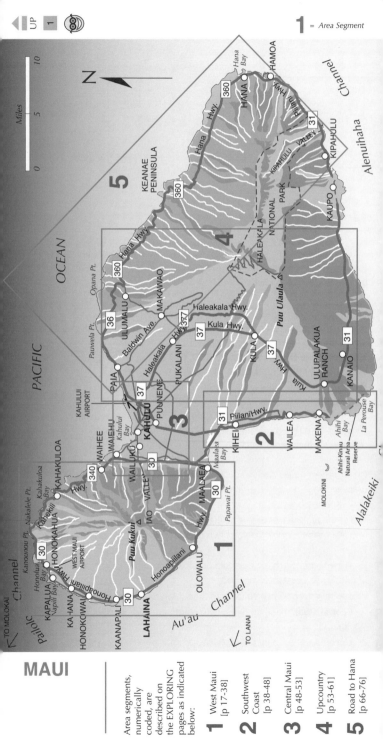

1 = *Area Segment*

MAUI

Area segments, numerically coded, are described on the EXPLORING pages as indicated below:

1 West Maui
[p 17-38]

2 Southwest Coast
[p 38-48]

3 Central Maui
[p 48-53]

4 Upcountry
[p 53-61]

5 Road to Hana
[p 66-76]

WEST MAUI | 1

Lahaina | Ka'anapali | Kapalua | West Maui's North Coast | Ma'alaea

Lahaina   *See Map 2 for Orientation*

A good place to begin your tour of West Maui—and Maui itself, we might suggest—is Lahaina, a colorful little town, situated on the west coast of Maui, just off Honoapi'ilani Highway (30), some 4 miles south of Ka'anapali Beach Resort. Lahaina is most notably a tourist mecca, filled with restaurants, shops and art galleries—of which there is a disproportionately large number here! Yet, this is also an historic town: during the early part of the 19th century it was the Royal Capital of Hawaii, from where King Kamehameha I—also known as Kamehameha the Great—ruled all the islands. In the early and mid 1800s, Lahaina became an important whaling port, overrun by lawless whalers, and a few years later, beginning in 1823, with the arrival of the first missionaries on the island—mostly from New England—the town became a prominent center for missionary activity. Relics from the missionary and whaling eras can still be seen here.

Exploring Front Street

Banyan Tree, Old Fort and Courthouse, Pioneer Inn, Baldwin House, Carthaginian

Lahaina's chief interest and visitor activity are of course centered on Front Street—near the waterfront—between Shaw Street and Lahainaluna Road, where most of the town's souvenir and T-shirt shops and art galleries are concentrated. Several of the town's most notable points of interest, too, are easily accessible from here. Just at the corner of Front and Hotel streets, for instance, you can search out the age-old **Banyan Tree**, quite possibly one of the town's **6** foremost tourist attractions. The tree is indeed quite spectacular, claimed to be the largest tree of its kind on the islands, covering almost an acre of land, with its branches extending nearly 50 yards, supported by aerial roots that grow downward into the ground to support the tree. The Banyan Tree was originally planted in 1873 by Lahaina Sheriff W.O. Smith, to commemorate the 50th anniversary of the arrival of the missionaries in Lahaina.

Nearby, on the harbor side of the Banyan Tree Square stands the **Old Courthouse**, originally built in 1857. It once served as the **5** center for government activities and housed a jail in its basement. The Courthouse and jail are now home to a couple of art galleries. Also of interest at the Banyan Tree Square, directly across from the waterfront, are the remnants of Lahaina's **Old Fort**, constructed from coral blocks in 1832. The fort was originally built to deter the rebellious whalers from the whaling ships anchored in the harbor, who were revolting against the town's newly-imposed disciplinary laws. Typically, cannons were mounted on the fort wall, and every night a King's soldier would beat a drum atop the fort, as a signal for all seamen to return to their ships or be confined to prison for the night. The fort was used primarily as a prison until 1854, at which time it was largely dismantled and the coral blocks taken to build the new town jail, Hale Pa'ahao.

2 Another place of supreme visitor interest, located on Front Street, adjacent to the Banyan Tree, is the historic **Pioneer Inn**, originally built in 1901, some 25 years after the end of the whaling era. It is, however, reflective, in its architecture and theme, of Lahaina's whaling period, with vintage whaling equipment and photographs of 19th-century whaling expeditions adorning its walls. The inn is believed to have been originally built at Keomuku, on the nearby island of Lanai, and later on barged across the channel to Lahaina. In any event, the 48-room inn, now largely restored, houses shops and a restaurant and saloon, and offers overnight guest accommodations.

3 Directly across from the Pioneer Inn, docked in the harbor and also well worth investigating, is the **Brig *Carthaginian***, which is in fact a replica—built in the 1920s—of the 19th-century square-riggers that brought the first missionaries from Boston, around the Horn, to Hawaii. The brig now houses a museum, with an exhibit on whales and whaling, and where you can also see films on whaling.

4 Close at hand, on the north side of Pioneer Inn, is the site of the **Brick Palace**, quite possibly the first Western structure on Maui, built by King Kamehameha I around 1800. Kamehameha was rather intrigued by Western architecture, as, too, he was with Western ships and weapons; but his favorite wife, Queen Ka'ahumanu, refused to live in the enclosed environment of the stone and brick structure, preferring, instead, a native Hawaiian grass hut located adjacent to the "palace." In any case, directly in front of the site of the Brick Palace, in the water, and also with some interest, is the Hauola Stone, bestowed, we are told, with magical healing powers.

1 For history buffs, there is yet another place of supreme interest. At the corner of Front and Dickenson streets, across from Pioneer Inn, stands the beautifully restored **Baldwin House**, built in the 1830s by missionary-physician Reverend Dwight Baldwin, who arrived in Lahaina in 1835,00 and lived and raised his family here, until his death in 1868. Reverend Baldwin conducted missionary activities as well as his medical practice from this house. The Baldwin House, constructed from coral and rock and plastered over, is now a living museum, filled with original furnishings and several personal and household items of the Baldwin family. The museum is operated by the Lahaina Restoration Foundation, origi-

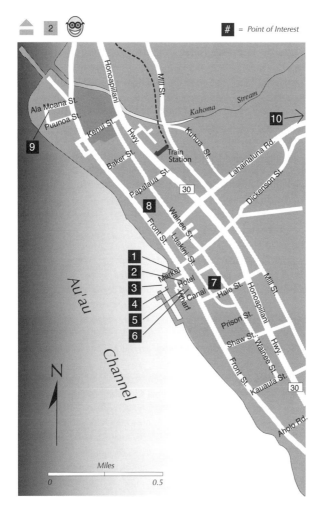

= *Point of Interest*

LAHAINA

1. Baldwin House
2. Pioneer Inn
3. Brig Carthaginian II
4. Site of Brick Palace
5. Old Fort and Courthouse
6. Banyan Tree
7. Hale Paahao Prison
8. Wo Hing Society Temple
9. Jodo Mission
10. Lahainaluna Seminary

nally established in the 1950s, and which has, over the years, rescued, restored and preserved many of Lahaina's historic buildings.

Adjacent to the Baldwin House, and also of interest, is the **Master's Reading Room**, where the Lahaina Restoration Foundation now has its offices. The Master's Reading Room, dating from 1833 and quite possibly Maui's oldest building, was originally used as storage space by missionaries, until, in 1834, the upper story was converted into an officers' club for masters and officers, providing in it also—as an added bonus—an excellent vantage point from where ships' captains could watch over their fleets and crews. The Reading Room, however, was sold at an auction, in 1846, to Reverend Baldwin, whose growing family then occupied it.

Farther Afield | *Hale Pa'ahao, Wailoa Church, Wo Hing Society Temple, Jodo Mission, Lahainaluna Seminary*

7 Try to also visit the new prison, **Hale Pa'ahao**—meaning "stuck-in-irons house"—located on Prison Street, at the corner of Waine'e Street. Hale Pa'ahao was originally built in 1854 from coral blocks taken from the Old Fort, and has been largely preserved in its original state, much as it appeared in the 1850s, with one cell displaying a mannequin of an old salt, and another a list of the convictions handed down over the years, posted on the wall, as well as the diary of an inmate confined to the cell.

South from Hale Pa'uhao on Waine'e Street, and also worth visiting, is the **Wailoa Congregational Church**, formerly the Waine'e Church, with its associations to Keopuolani, wife to Kamehameha I and mother of Kamehameha II and Kamehameha III, who was one of the first Hawaiians to convert to Christianity at this church. The church, it is interesting to note, was originally built in 1823 and subsequently destroyed and rebuilt several times over the years, the last in 1988, when it was renamed, Wailoa, meaning "living waters." There is a cemetery, the Wailoa Cemetery, located adjacent to the church, where several members of Hawaii's royal family are buried, as well as some early missionaries and their children.

A little way from the Wailoa Church, at the corner of Front and Shaw streets, is the Malu'uluolele Park, a community park with a baseball facility and basketball and tennis courts. Interestingly, the park is also the site of the ancient Mokuhinia Pond, which at one time featured a small islet at the center of it, where the royal residences of Kamehameha II and, later on, Kamehameha III once stood. The pond also, we are told, was once the home of Hawaii's legendary *mo'o* (lizard), Kilawahine, which visited all the Hawaiian islands, unifying the bloodlines of all the islands' inhabitants.

Another place of interest, northward from the center of town, on
8 Front Street, is the **Wo Hing Society Temple**, dating from 1812, and originally built as a fraternal and social meeting hall for Hawaii's Chinese population. The temple now houses a museum devoted

to Chinese culture, exhibiting Chinese artifacts, including a Taoist shrine located on its upper floor. There is also a small, historic theater located adjacent to the temple, the Cookhouse Theatre, which features some fascinating old films of Hawaii, shot by Thomas Edison in 1898.

Just to the north of the center of town, too, about a mile or so on Ala Moana Street, stands the **Jodo Mission**, which has in it one of the largest statues of Buddha outside Asia. The statue was erected in 1968 to commemorate the centennial of the arrival of the first Japanese immigrants in Hawaii in 1868.

Yet another place of interest, eastward from the center of town of Lahaina, some 2 miles on Lahainaluna Road, which goes off Honoapi'ilani Highway, is the historic **Lahainaluna Seminary**. The seminary was founded in 1831 by missionaries, and has the distinction of being the oldest educational institution in the West. It also has in it one of the oldest printing presses west of the Rockies, the Hale Pai—literally translated, the "House of Printing"—on which, in 1834, the first Hawaiian-language newspaper was printed, as well as texts used at the seminary. Hale Pai now has on display a replica of the original press, as well as the original oak plates and samples of the early type, including some first editions of books printed here in the 1830s.

Interestingly, one of Lahainaluna's most notable graduates was David Malo, acknowledged as Hawaii's first scholar, who also wrote the definitive Hawaiian history, *Hawaiian Antiquities*. Malo foresaw and feared the changing of the Hawaiian culture, and asked to be buried "high above the tide of foreign invasion." His grave can now be seen on the hillside, by the giant "L," above Lahainaluna.

Ka'anapali

Sugarcane Train,
Whaler's Village
and Resorts

  See Map 3
for Orientation

From Lahaina, it is 4 miles directly north on the coastal Honoapi'ilani Highway (30) to Ka'anapali, passing by, approximately midway between Lahaina and Ka'anapali, two roadside beach parks—Wahikuli State Wayside Beach Park and Hanakao'o Beach Park—both with good swimming and snorkeling possibilities, and the latter especially popular with beach goers.

Alternatively, you can journey to Ka'anapali on board the Lahaina-Ka'anapali & Pacific Railroad—popularly known as the Sugarcane Train—a 19th-century steam train that once transported sugar from a Lahaina mill to a warehouse just to the north of Black Rock, in Ka'anapali, from where it was then shipped out by boat. The Sugarcane Train now whisks tourists through cane fields, through an area between Lahaina and Ka'anapali that was once devoted entirely to the cultivation of sugarcane. The **Sugarcane Train**

12 **Station** in Lahaina, by the way, is located just north of Lahainaluna Road—which goes off Honoapi'ilani Highway (30)—on Hinau Road.

In any event, Ka'anapali is one of Hawaii's most popular beach resorts—second only to Oahu's Waikiki—and also the western most point on Maui. The Ka'anapali Beach itself is a glorious, 3-mile-long white-sand beach, bordered by world-class, luxury high-rise hotels and condominium complexes, developed mostly between 1962 and 1987. There are, in fact, six full-fledged hotels here—Hyatt Regency, Westin, Sheraton, Marriott, Ka'anapali Beach Hotel and Royal Lahaina—five condominium complexes, two championship, 18-hole golf courses, dozens of tennis courts, a first-class shopping mall, and several excellent restaurants.

Prominent among Ka'anapali's properties is of course the splen-
3 did, 815-room **Hyatt Regency Maui**, sprawled over 18½ acres at the southern end of the Ka'anapali Beach Resort, and developed, in 1980, by Hawaii's famous developer, Chris Hemmeter, at a cost of around $80 million. The hotel boasts five restaurants and six bars, a dazzling lobby with a century-old banyan tree, acres of well-kept gardens—filled with tropical plants, trees and flowers, and exotic birds such as peacocks, penguins, flamingos and swans—lagoons, a half-acre swimming pool with a 2½-story-high water slide, and some 60 waterfalls, large and small. The hotel also has on display a superb, $2-million art collection, featuring Hawaiian and South Pacific art and rare antiques.

Just to the north of the Hyatt Regency, on a 15-acre site, sits
4 the **Maui Marriott**, a 720-room, 9-story hotel, with an open-air lobby that rises four full stories, developed in 1981; and north of
2 there, situated on the beach, is the **Westin Maui**, the other gem of Ka'anapali, with its two 11-story towers and 761 ocean view rooms, also developed by Chris Hemmeter. The Westin, in fact, was formerly the Maui Surf Hotel, redeveloped in 1987 at a cost of $155 million. It now features 9 restaurants and lounges, landscaped grounds with exotic birds, 5 multi-level swimming pools, water slides, more than a dozen waterfalls, and an extensive $2.5 million collection of Asian and Pacific art.

Among Ka'anapali's other hotels, lying farther to the north along
5 Ka'anapali Beach, are the low-rise, 429-room **Ka'anapali Beach**
6 **Hotel**; the 503-room **Sheraton-Maui**, situated on a 23-acre site, and originally developed in 1963; and the 12-story, 545-room **Royal**
7 **Lahaina**, the oldest of Ka'anapali's hotels, built in December, 1962.

Besides the resorts, there is more to interest the visitor at Ka'anapali. More or less at the center of the Ka'anapali strip, for instance,
1 lies the **Whaler's Village**, an outdoor shopping mall with more than 50 shops and restaurants, and—equally important at Ka'anapali—ample parking. A place of special interest at the Whaler's Village is the Whaling Museum, which has some excellent exhibits depicting life during the whaling era, including old photographs, whaling

WEST MAUI | Ka'anapali

= Point of Interest

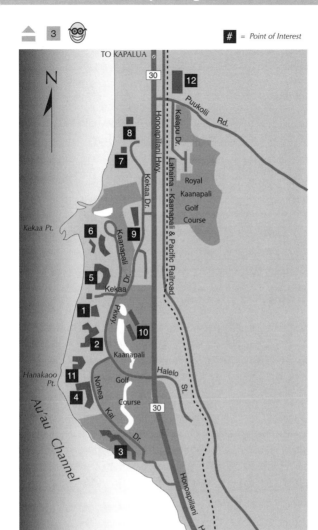

KA'ANAPALI

1. Whaler's Village
2. Westin Maui
3. Hyatt Regency
4. Maui Marriott
5. Kaanapali Beach Hotel
6. Sheraton Maui
7. Royal Lahaina
8. Maui Kaanapali Villas
9. Maui Eldorado Resort
10. Kaanapali Royal Hotel
11. Kaanapali Alii
12. Train Station

WEST MAUI | Kapalua

artifacts, and films on the history of Maui's whaling industry.

Another place of interest, at the north end of Ka'anapali Beach, near the Sheraton-Maui, is Black Rock, known to the Hawaiians as a Leina a Kauhane, meaning "soul's leap." Black Rock is in many ways a sacred place where, according to Hawaiian legend, the dying would enter the world of spirits by leaping off the cliffs into the ocean below. The Black Rock area, we might add, also offers some of the best swimming and snorkeling at Maui, especially in calm weather.

Ka'anapali's white-sand beach continues beyond Black Rock, northward, offering good swimming possibilities and also fewer people. To access this northern part of the beach, you can either walk around Black Rock or go north from Ka'anapali on Honoapi'ilani Highway, about a mile, then take Pu'ukolii Road off the highway, toward the ocean, and follow the signs to the beach.

| **Kapalua** | *Kapalua Bay Hotel, D.T. Fleming Beach* | | *See Map 4 for Orientation* |

North from Ka'anapali, the high-rise resort development quickly gives way to smaller beach communities—Honokowai and Kahana—cluttered with low-rise condominium complexes, mostly two and three stories high, and situated on Lower Honoapi'ilani Road that runs parallel to Honoapi'ilani Highway to the west, closer to the coast. The beaches along here, too, are smaller and less attractive than, say, Ka'anapali Beach to the south, or those farther to the north, at Napili and Kapalua; however, the Honokowai-Kahana coast offers good, unobstructed views of the nearby islands of Lanai and Molokai. Besides which, as an added bonus for the budget-minded traveler, the area, quite typically, offers more affordable accommodations than the Ka'anapali and Kapalua resorts.

Farther still, north of Honokowai and Kahana, a mile or two, lies Napili Bay, which has a delightful, palm-fringed, white-sand beach, with excellent swimming and snorkeling possibilities and superb views, across the Pailolo Channel, of Molokai. Napili Bay also offers good golf—at nearby Kapalua—and tennis facilities, as well as some shopping possibilities and one or two worthwhile restaurants.

Adjoining to the north of Napili Bay is Kapalua, one of West Maui's most prestigious resorts, originally developed in the mid-1970s by the Maui Land & Pineapple Company. The resort is largely built around the lovely, crescent-shaped, white-sand beach of the same name, Kapalua Beach, which, again, offers excellent swimming and snorkeling possibilities. The centerpiece of the resort is of course the exclusive—and, yes, expensive—194-room **Kapalua Bay Hotel**, that, needless to say, has commanding views of the ocean on nearly all sides, backing onto a wooded, 18-hole golf course and, happily, fields of pineapple. There are also tennis courts here, and first-class shops and restaurants. In addition to which, the Kapalua Resort includes in it two luxury condominium complexes, the 118-unit Kapalua Villas and the 40-unit Ironwoods.

Northeastward from Kapalua on Honoapi'ilani Highway, a mile or so—past mile marker 31—is Honokahua Bay, at the head of which lies the **D.T. Fleming Beach Park**, a popular beach, named for David T. Fleming, a manager at the nearby Honolua Ranch in the early 1900s, and who, most notably, helped introduce pineapple as a commercial crop in West Maui. The beach has picnic tables, showers and restrooms; occasionally, it also offers surfing possibilities, though swimming is not encouraged here due to the strong undercurrents that make it rather unsafe. Near the beach, too, behind the sand dunes just to the south, is an ancient Hawaiian burial site where skeletal remains were unearthed when construction began on a new hotel. The hotel—Ritz Carlton—subsequently relocated to a site farther inland, and the burial site is now being restored.

West Maui's North Coast   4 See Map 4 for Orientation

Honokahua | Mokuleia Beach Honolua-Mokuleia Marine Life Preserve, Honolua Bay

The coastal stretch north from Honokahua Bay to Honokohau Bay, and, again, from Honokohau Bay southeastward toward Wailuku, is rather lovely, largely unspoiled and remarkably picturesque, with rugged cliffs overhanging the ocean and lush valleys and pasture lands fanning out inland, and breathtaking views to be encountered at every turn of the highway (which, here, is still the Honoapi'ilani Highway). Indeed, the coastal stretch along here offers the motorist-adventurer a rare opportunity to experience pristine Hawaii.

In any case, first off, a little over a mile from Honokahua Bay—just past mile marker 32—and reached by way of a small trail leading from the highway turnout down to the ocean, is **Mokuleia Beach**, popularly known as Slaughterhouse Beach, for its treacherous waves that, particularly during the winter months, can be seen vengefully pounding the small, sandy beach below. Mokuleia, nevertheless, as locals will tell you, is *the* place for bodysurfing during the summer months.

Mokuleia Beach itself lies at the head of Mokuleia Bay, adjoining to the north of which is Honolua Bay, which together form the **Honolua-Mokuleia Bay Marine Life Conservation District**, a preserve where removal or molestation of any marine life, shell rocks or corals is prohibited, making this an excellent area for snorkeling, especially in calm weather. Interestingly, it is also possible to snorkel or swim from one bay to the other, around Kalaepiha Point, which separates the two bays.

Honolua Bay is also one of Hawaii's foremost surfing spots—second only to Oahu's North Shore—that has been featured on several surfing posters and covers of surfing magazines. For spectators, there is Lipoa Point—reached by way of a dirt trail that dashes off the highway, a half-mile or so past mile marker 33, and journeys along the east side of the bay to the top of the headland—which has a bird's-eye view of the bay below, and from where you can watch world-class surfers challenge some of the most spectacular waves, particularly during the winter months.

Three miles from Honolua Bay on Honoapi'ilani Highway, northeastward, and we are at Honokohau Bay, which has very little of interest, save for a small, rocky beach that attracts a handful of surfers. Honokohau Bay is nonetheless important in that it marks the end of Honoapi'ilani Highway (30) and the beginning of Kahekili Highway (340), the latter of which journeys along the backside of West Maui, skirting the West Maui Mountains to the northeast, some 22 miles southeastward to Wailuku, taking in at least 2 miles of unpaved road that can often be impassable, particularly during wet weather.

| East to Waiehu | Nakele Light Station, Blowhole, Pohaku Kani, Waihe'e and Waiehu Beaches, Halekii-Pihana Heiaus |

At any rate, 2 miles or so eastward from Honokohau Bay on Kahekili Highway (340), a small side road—accessed only on foot—dashes off toward the ocean, to the **Nakalele Light Station**, situated on a grassy slope—ideally suited to picnicking and strolling around—that tumbles down to the cliffs, at the bottom of which you can see a series of rock arches and natural pools. Also of interest, some 2½ miles from the light station, just off the highway, on the ocean side, is a lookout that has good views of a **blowhole**. South from the blowhole, another 1½ miles, the paved road finally ends, and a little way from there, a half mile or so, just off the highway, with a rusty old sign pointing to it, is **Pohaku Kani**—the Bellstone—a six-foot-high boulder, which, we are told, if struck in a certain manner, can resound throughout the adjacent valley.

Farther still, a little over a mile, at Kahakuloa—a tiny fishing village with a handful of houses, *taro* patches, and two or three churches—the paved road begins again. From Kahakuloa, it is another 7 miles or so to the "Maluhia Camp" turnoff, from where a narrow, mile-long side road leads through rolling pastures to **Waihe'e Trailhead**, at the head of the 3-mile-long Waihe'e Ridge Trail, that in turn leads to Lanilili peak, elevation 2,563 feet. The trail is somewhat challenging, climbing roughly 1,500 feet over the 3 miles, but well worth the effort, with good, all-round views to be enjoyed from the top.

Some 2 miles southeastward from the Waihe'e Trail turnoff, on the *makai* side of the highway, is Waihe'e Point, which has superb views of the coastline below, and south of there are the sleepy little

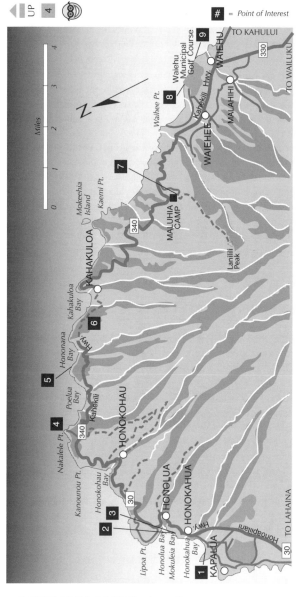

= Point of Interest

WEST MAUI'S NORTH COAST

1. D.T. Fleming Beach
2. Honolua-Mokuleia Bay
   Marine Life
   Conservation District
3. Mokuleia Beach
4. Nakalele Light Station
5. Blowhole
6. Pohaku Kani
   (Bellstone)
7. Waihee Trailhead
8. Waihee Beach
9. Waiehu Beach

towns of Waihe'e—about a mile from Waihe'e Point—and Waiehu, another 2 miles or so from Waihe'e. **Waihe'e** and **Waiehu** each have a **beach park**, frequented primarily by fishermen, and a golf course situated more or less midway between the two towns.

From Waiehu, Kahekili Highway heads directly south to Wailuku, passing by, just to the north of Wailuku, the **Halekii-Pihana Heiaus State Monument**—reached by way of Waiehu Beach Road that goes off the highway, then Kuhio Place southwestward, off Waiehu Beach Road, and Hea Place south off Kuhio Place to Halekii Heiau, the first of the two *heiaus*, set on small hill by the Iao Stream; and Pihana Heiau, situated just to the south of Halekii Heiau, at the end of a short trail. The *heiaus* are historically significant, in that Maui's King Kahekili once lived here, and also Queen Kepuolani, wife of Kamehameha I and mother of Kamehameha II, was born here. From the Halekii-Pihana *heiaus*, you can return to Waiehu Beach Road or the Kahekili Highway, both important arteries, and so to Wailuku.

Lahaina to Ma'alaea

It is approximately 15 miles from Lahaina south to Ma'alaea, journeying along West Maui's south coast on Honoapi'ilani Highway (30), with the West Maui Mountains on one side and the ocean on the other. The coastal stretch, quite typically, is dotted with a handful of small beach parks—many of which offer swimming, snorkeling and picnicking possibilities—and one or two lookouts, adding to the interest of the motorist. From Ma'alaea it is another 6 miles or so northward, across the isthmus, to Wailuku, in East Maui.

In any case, northernmost on the route, a mile or so south from Lahaina, is the Puamana Beach Park, a grassy park with a narrow strip of sand, which offers good swimming and, occasionally, surfing possibilities; and a mile south of there lies Launiupoko State Wayside Park, which has a small sandy beach, a man-made children's wading pool, picnic tables, barbecue grills, and showers and restrooms. The Launiupoko park also has excellent views of the islands of Lanai and Kaho'olawe, just to the west and south, respectively.

Some 3 miles farther southeastward lies Olowalu, a village, no more, notable as the site of the 1790 Olowalu Massacre, which resulted when a longboat was stolen from an American ship by Hawaiians, primarily for its iron content, and in retaliation the American captain, Simon Metcalf, tricked the Hawaiians into approaching his ship and opened fire on them, killing more than a hundred natives. Olowalu now has in it a general store and a French restaurant, Chez Paul. Besides which, a small cane road leads from here—from near the water tank located behind the general store—a half-mile *mauka*—toward the mountains—to some petroglyphs depicting human figures and various animals.

South from Olowalu, another mile or so, lies Punahoa Beach, an essentially undeveloped roadside beach, bordered by native *kiawe* trees. Punahoa has some good snorkeling and, occasionally, surfing possibilities.

Just to the south of Punahoa Beach, 2 miles, is Ukumehame Beach Park, with its narrow, rocky coastal strip, frequented primarily by fishermen; and another half-mile south of there, situated just off the highway, is Papalaua State Wayside Park, also undeveloped, and backing onto groves of *kiawe*. The Papalaua beach park offers picnicking and surfing possibilities.

Farther still, another 3 miles southeastward, and we are at Papawai Point, the southernmost point on West Maui, where there is a lookout with good views of Molokini and Kaho'olawe to the south and Haleakala farther to the southeast. Papawai Point, we might add, is also an excellent place for whale watching during season—November to May—from where you can see the humpback whales and their calves frolicking in the ocean just off shore.

Finally, some 3 or 4 miles farther, as the highway turns northeastward, there is Ma'alaea, a small boat harbor from where you can take boat excursions or fishing trips out to sea. From Ma'alaea, too, you can continue northward on Honoapi'ilani Highway to Wailuku, or return to Lahaina via the same route.

Accommodations | Lahaina, Ka'anapali, Kapalua

Aston Ka'anapali Shores. *$240-$395.* 3445 Honoapi'ilani Hwy., Ka'anapali; (808) 667-2211/(800) 922-7866/(800) 321-2558 in Hawaii/*www.astonhotels.com*. 427 oceanfront condominium units, with TV, phones, air-conditioning, and kitchen facilities. Swimming pool, tennis court, restaurant and cocktail lounge, meeting rooms, shops. Daily maid service.

Aston Pake Maui. *$180-$395.* 3615 Lower Honoapi'ilani Hwy., Lahaina; (808) 669-8235/(800) 922-7866/(877) 997-6667/*www. astonhotels.com*. 112 studio and 1- and 2-bedroom condominium units, with TV, phones, ceiling fans, kitchens, and maid service. Swimming pool. Handicapped facilities.

Embassy Suites Resort. *$210-$450.* 104 Ka'anapali Shores Place, Honokowai; (808) 661-2000/(800) 669-3155/*www.embassysuites.hilton.com*. 413-unit resort, located on the beach. TV, phones, mini kitchens, and air-conditioning. Swimming pool, health club, spa; restaurant and cocktail lounge, meeting rooms, shops. Handicapped facilities.

Garden Gate Bed & Breakfast. $109-$129. 67 Kaniau Rd.,

Lahaina; (808) 661-8800/(800) 939-3217/*www.gardengatebb.com*. Located near beach. Offers 4 guest rooms with TV, phones and air-conditioning. Hearty country breakfast. Minimum stay, 3 days.

Hale Kai Condominiums. *$115-$225*. 3691 Lower Honoapi'ilani Hwy., Honokowai; (808) 669-6333/(800) 446-7307*www.halekai. com*. 40 oceanfront condominium units, with TV, phones, ceiling fans and kitchenettes. Swimming pool. Maid service. Minimum stay: 3 days.

Hyatt Regency Maui. *$295-$525*. 200 Nohea Kai Dr., Ka'anapali; (808) 661-1234/(800) 233-1234/*www.hyatt.com*. 815-room luxury resort hotel. Facilities include swimming pools, health club and spa, tennis courts, golf course, restaurants and cocktail lounges, meeting rooms, and shops and beauty salon. Handicapped facilities.

Ka'anapali Ali'i. *$360-$760*. 50 Nohea Kai Dr., Ka'anapali; (808) 667-1400/(800) 642-MAUI (642-6284)/*www.classicresorts. com*. 210 oceanfront condominium units, with TV, phones, air-conditioning, and kitchens. Also swimming pool, health club and spa, and tennis courts. Daily maid service. Minimum stay, 3 days.

Ka'anapali Beach Hotel. *$175-$525*. 2525 Ka'anapali Pkwy., Ka'anapali; (808) 661-0011/(800) 262-8450/*www.kbhmaui.com*. Beach front hotel with 430 units with TV, phones, and air-conditioning. Swimming pool, restaurants and cocktail lounge, meeting rooms, shops and beauty salon. Handicapped facilities.

Ka'anapali Royal. *$150-$220*. 2560 Keka'a Dr., Ka'anapali; (808) 667-7200/*www.kaanapaliroyal.com*. 105 condominium units, with TV, phones, kitchen facilities, air-conditioning, and daily maid service. Swimming pool, tennis courts, golf course. Handicapped facilities. Minimum stay, 2 nights.

Kahana Sunset. *$135-$380*. 4909 Lower Honoapi'ilani Hwy., Kahana; (808) 669-0423/(800) 332-1137/*www.kapalua.com*. 71 condominium units on the beach. TV, phones, kitchens; also swimming pool. Daily maid service. Minimum stay, 3 days.

Kapalua Bay Hotel & Villas. *$225-$500*. One Bay Dr., Kapalua; (808) 669-5656/(800) 367-8000/*www.kapaluabayhotel.com*. Luxury, oceanfront resort, with 196 ocean view rooms and suites and 14 oceanfront villas, situated on 750 acres. Facilities include swimming pools, tennis courts, golf courses, restaurants and cocktail lounge, shops, and beauty salon. Handicapped facilities.

Kapalua Villas. *$209-$585*. 500 Office Road, Kapalua; (808) 669-8808/(800) 545-0018/*www.kapaluavillas.com*. Offers 1, 2 and 3-bedroom condominium villas, situated on scenic, landscaped grounds. Fairway, ocean view and oceanfront settings. Facilities at nearby Kapalua Bay Hotel are available to all guests at the villas.

Kulakane. *$145-$250*. 3741 Lower Honoapi'ilani Rd., Honokowai; (808) 669-6119/(800) 367-6088/*www.kulakane.com*. 42 condominium units with ocean views; TV, phones, kitchens, maid service. Swimming pool. Minimum stay: 3 days.

Lahaina Inn. *$125-$205*. 127 Lahainaluna Rd., Lahaina; (808) 661-0577/(800) 669-3444/*www.lahainainn.com*. 13-unit, turn-of-the-century boutique hotel, situated in the center of Lahaina township. Guest rooms feature private lanais. Continental breakfast.

Lahaina Shores Beach Resort. *$185-$325*. 475 Front St., Lahaina: (808) 661-4835/(800) 628-6699/*www.classicresorts.com*. 199-unit beach front resort. TV, phones, kitchens, and air-conditioning. Swimming pool. Daily maid service. Handicapped facilities.

Mahana at Ka'anapali. *$199-$675*. 110 Ka'anapali Shore Pl., Ka'anapali; (808) 661-8751/(800) 922-7866/(800) 321-2558 in Hawaii/*www.astonhotels.com*. 215 ocean-view condominium units, with TV and phones, air-conditioning, and full kitchens. Swimming pool, tennis courts. Handicapped facilities. Minimum stay: 3 days.

Maui Islander Hotel. *$99-$199*. 660 Waine'e St., Lahaina; (808) 667-9766/(800) 367-5226/(800) 542-6827 in Hawaii/*www.ohana.com*. 360 units, with TV, phones, and air-conditioning; some kitchen facilities. Swimming pool, tennis court. Handicapped facilities.

Maui Ka'anapali Villas. *$150-$490*. 45 Kai Ala Dr., Ka'anapali; (808) 667-7791/(800) 922-7866/(800) 321-2558 in Hawaii/*www.astonhotels.com*. Beach front condominium complex with 250 units. TV, phones, air-conditioning, kitchens. Also swimming pool and shops on premises. Maid service. Handicapped facilities.

Marriott's Maui Ocean Club. *$295-$510*. 100 Nohea Kai Dr., Ka'anapali; (808) 667-1200/(800) 763-1333/*www.marriott.com*. 720-room full-service resort hotel, located on Ka'anapali Beach. Hotel facilities include swimming pools, health club, tennis courts, golf courses, restaurants and cocktail lounge, shops, and beauty salon. Handicapped facilities.

Mauian Hotel. *$125-$195*. 5441 Honoapi'ilani Rd., Napili; (808) 669-6205/(800) 367-5034/*www.mauian.com*. 44 studio apartments, fronting on Napili Bay. TV and phones; kitchens, ceiling fans. Swimming pool and meeting rooms.

Napili Kai Beach Resort. *$200-$760*. 5900 Honoapi'ilani Rd., Napili: (808) 669-6271/(800) 367-5030/*www.napilikai.com*. 165-unit condominium complex, located on Napili Bay. TV, phones, kitchens; swimming pools, tennis courts, restaurant and cocktail lounge, and shops. Handicapped facilities.

Napili Point Resort. *$195-$430*. 5295 Honoapi'ilani Hwy., Napili; (808) 669-9222/(800) 669-6252/*www.napili.com*. 115 oceanfront condominium units, with TV, phones, and kitchens. Swimming pools. Daily maid service.

Napili Sunset. *$120-$255*. 46 Hui Dr., Napili; (808) 669-80837(800) 447-9229/*www.napilisunset.com*. Beach front condominium complex with 42 units with TV and phones. Swimming pool. Maid service. Minimum stay, 3 days.

Napili Surf Beach Resort. *$140-$299*. 50 Napili Pl., Napili;

(808) 669-8002/(800) 541-0638/*www.napilisurf.com*. 54 beach front condominium units, with TV, and kitchens. Swimming pools; maid service. Minimum stay: 5 days.

Napili Village. *$99-$139*. 5425 Lower Honoapi'ilani Hwy., Napili; (808) 669-6228/(800) 336-2185/*www.napilivillage.com*. 30 condominium units, with TV and kitchens. Swimming pool, beauty salon, and shops. Short walk to beach. Minimum stay: 3 days.

Noelani Condominium Resort. *$157-$237*. 4095 Lower Honoapi'ilani Rd., Kahana; (808) 669-8374/(800) 367-6030/*www.noelani-condo-resort.com*. 50 units in oceanfront condominium complex. TV, phones, and kitchens. Swimming pools. Minimum stay: 3 days.

Outrigger Maui Eldorado. *$145-$480*. 2661 Keka'a Dr.. Ka'anapali; (808) 922-9700/(888) 339-8585/(800) 219-9700 in Hawaii/*www.outrigger.com*. 204 oceanfront studios and 1- and 2-bedroom condominium units, with TV, phones, air-conditioning, kitchens, and washer and dryer. Swimming pool and shops on premises. Daily maid service.

Outrigger Napili Shores. *$119-$245*. 5315 Lower Honoapi'ilani Rd., Napili; (808) 669-8061/(888) 859-7867/*www.outrigger.com*. 114 studio and 1-bedroom condominium units on Napili Beach. TV, phones, ceiling fans, kitchens. Swimming pools, heated spa, restaurant and cocktail lounge on premises. Daily maid service.

Outrigger Royal Kahana. *$145-485*. 4365. Lower Honoapi'ilani Rd., Napili; (808) 669-5911/(800)447-7783/*www.outrigger.com*. 198 oceanfront 1- and 2-bedroom condominium units. TV, phones, air-conditioning, kitchens, and washer and dryer. Swimming pool. Maid service. Handicapped facilities.

Pioneer Inn. *$125-$165*. 658 Wharf St., Lahaina; (808) 667-5708/(800) 457-5457/*www.pioneerinnmaui.com*. 48 rooms in historic inn, built in 1901. Restaurant and bar on premises, with live entertainment. Located in the center of town.

Plantation Inn. *$160-$265*. 174 Lahainaluna Rd., Lahaina; (808) 667-9225/(800) 433-6815/*www.theplantationinn.com*. Country-style inn with 19 guest rooms and suites; TV, phones, air-conditioning. Swimming pool, restaurants and cocktail lounge. Maid service. Minimum stay: 3 days.

Polynesian Shores. *$135-$245*. 3975 Lower Honoapi'ilani Hwy., Honokowai; (808) 669-60657(800) 433-6284/*www.polynesianshores.com*. 52 oceanfront condominium units, with TV, phones, and full kitchens. Swimming pool. Minimum stay, 3 days.

Ritz Carlton. *$285-$2,800*. 1 Ritz Carlton Dr., Kapalua; (808) 669-6200/(800) 262-8440/*www.ritzcarlton.com*. 550-room luxury resort hotel with ocean and mountain view rooms with marble bathrooms. Facilities include a swimming pool, health club, spa, golf course and tennis courts; also restaurants and cocktail lounge.

Royal Lahaina Resort. *$195-$550*. 2780 Keka'a Dr., Ka'anapali;

(808) 661-3611/(800) 447-6925/*www.hawaiihotels.com*. Beach front hotel with 516 units. TV, phones, some kitchens. Swimming pools, tennis courts and golf course. Restaurant and cocktail lounge, meeting rooms, and shops and beauty salon on premises. Handicapped facilities.

Sands of Kahana. *$185-$410.* 4299 Lower Honoapi'ilani Rd., Kahana; (808) 669-0423/(800) 326-9874/(800) 332-1137/*www. kapalua.com*. 196 beach front condominium units, with TV, phones, and kitchens. Swimming pool, health club with spa, and restaurants and cocktail lounge.

Sheraton Maui Hotel. *$395-$505.* 2605 Ka'anapali Pkwy., Ka'anapali; (808) 661-0031/(800) 325-3535/*www.sheraton.com*. 492-room full-service resort hotel, situated on Ka'anapali Beach. Facilities include swimming pool, tennis courts, golf course, restaurant and cocktail lounge, meeting rooms, and shops. Handicapped facilities.

The Westin Maui Resort. *$269-$495.* 2365 Ka'anapali Pkwy., Ka'anapali; (808) 667-2525/(800) 228-3000/*www.westin.com*. Luxury resort hotel with 761 rooms and suites, fronting on Ka'anapali Beach. Hotel facilities include swimming pools, health club and spa, restaurants and cocktail lounges, shops and beauty salon. Handicapped facilities.

The Whaler on Ka'anapali Beach. *$190-$600.* 2481 Ka'anapali Pkwy., Ka'anapali; (808) 661-4861/(800) 922-7866/(877) 977-6667/ *www.astonhotels.com*. 340-unit beach front resort. TV and phones, air-conditioning, kitchens. Swimming pool, health club and spa, and meeting rooms. Daily maid service. Handicapped facilities.

Dining | Lahaina, Ka'anapali, Kapalua

[Restaurant prices—based on full course dinner, excluding drinks, tax and tips—are categorized as follows: *Deluxe,* over $30, *Expensive,* $20-$30; *Moderate,* $10-$20; *Inexpensive,* under $10.]

The Banyan Tree. *Expensive-Deluxe.* One Ritz-Carlton Dr., Kapalua; (808) 669-6200/*www.ritzcarlton.com*. Ocean view restaurant with spectacular view of Molokai and the Paliolo Channel. Features contemporary Australian cuisine with French, Japanese and local influences. Four-course menu includes seafood, poultry, duck, lamb and beef. Live Pacific Islands music. Open for dinner. Reservations recommended.

Basil and Tomatoes Italian Grille. *Moderate-Expensive.* At the Royal Lahaina Resort, 2780 Keka'a Dr. Ka'anapali, (808) 662-3210. Casual, open-air restaurant, overlooking the Ka'anapali North Golf Course and Maui coastline, serving seafood and Italian dishes, with

WEST MAUI | Dining

an emphasis on fresh Hawaiian ingredients. Open for dinner daily.

The Bay Club. *Expensive.* At the Kapalua Bay Hotel, One Bay Dr., Kapalua; (808) 669-5656/669-8008. Well-appointed ocean-view restaurant, offering guests some of the most breathtaking sunsets. Serves primarily fresh island seafood. Menu selections include cured salmon sashimi, lobster, and mahi mahi with tropical fruit salsa. Open for dinner daily. Reservations recommended.

The Beach Club. *Moderate.* At the Aston Ka'anapali Shores, 3445 Lower Honoapi'ilani Hwy., Ka'anapali; (808) 667-2211/. Family-style restaurant in oceanfront setting. Continental cuisine, with emphasis on fresh seafood. Also live Hawaiian and contemporary music. Open for breakfast, lunch and dinner daily.

Beach Rock. *Inexpensive-Moderate.* At the Maui Marriott Resort, 100 Nohea Kai Dr., Ka'anapali; (808) 667-1200. Pool side snack bar serving sandwiches, salads, burgers and cocktails. Open for breakfast and lunch.

Bubba Gump Shrimp Company. *Moderate.* 889 Front St., Lahaina; (808) 661-3111/www.bubbagump.com. Waterfront restaurant, offering good views of Kaho'olawe, Molokai and Lanai, and memorable sunsets. Menu features seafood, steak, prime rib and chicken. Open for lunch and dinner daily.

Buzz's Wharf. *Expensive.* 50 Hauoli St., Ma'alaea Bay; (808) 244-5426. Situated at the Ma'alaea Harbor, with superb views of the ocean, Kihei and Mt. Haleakala. Offers primarily fresh island seafood and steak. Lunch and dinner daily. Reservations suggested.

Canoe's Restaurant. *Moderate.* 1450 Front St., Lahaina; (808) 661-0937. Established restaurant, quite popular with sunset-watchers. Specialties include fresh seafood, steak and prime rib. Open for lunch and dinner. Reservations suggested.

Cascades Grill and Sushi Bar. *Moderate.* At the Hyatt Regency Maui, Napili Tower, Ka'anapali; (808) 661-1234. Open-air setting. Serves primarily fresh island fish and seafood. Also full sushi bar. Open for dinner daily. Reservations suggested.

Chez Paul. *Expensive.* Hwy. 30, Olowalu Village; (808) 661-3843. One of the best-known French restaurants in Maui, offering classic French cuisine. Elegant decor. Dinners at 6.30 p.m. and 8.30 p.m. Reservations recommended.

Compadres Mexican Bar & Grill. *Moderate.* 1221 Honoapi'ilani Hwy., The Cannery Mall, Lahaina; (808)661-7189. Authentic Mexican food, including grilled fajitas and seafood entrees featuring fresh island fish. Breakfast, lunch and dinner daily.

David Paul's Lahaina Grill. *Deluxe.* At the Lahaina Hotel. 127 Lahainaluna Rd., Lahaina; (808) 667-5117/www.lahainagrill.com. Elegant restaurant, serving "New American Cuisine," including European, Asian and southwestern dishes. Open for lunch and dinner. Reservations recommended.

The Gardenia Court. *Moderate-Expensive.* At the Kapalua Bay

Hotel, One Bay Dr., Kapalua; (808) 669-5656. Open-air setting, amid lush tropical plants and waterways, with panoramic ocean views. International cuisine, featuring two buffets: a prime rib buffet on Wednesday nights and a seafood buffet on Friday nights. Open for breakfast and dinner, Mon.-Sat.; also Sunday brunch. Reservations recommended.

Gerard's Restaurant. *Deluxe.* At the Plantation Inn, 174 Lahainaluna Rd., Lahaina; (808) 661-8939/(877) 661-8939/*www. gerardsmaui.com.* French restaurant, serving fresh seafood and veal and lamb preparations with local seasonings; also poultry. Extensive dessert menu. Open for dinner daily. Reservations suggested.

Giovanni's Ristorante. *Moderate.* Ka'anapali Parkway. Ka'anapali; (808) 661-3160. Casual, family-style restaurant, serving gourmet pizza, seafood, pasta and vegetarian dishes. Open for dinner daily.

Hard Rock Cafe. *Moderate.* 900 Front St., Lahaina; (808) 667-7400/*www.hardrockcafe.com.* Casual, garden-style ocean view restaurant, decorated with rock 'n roll and surfer memorabilia, with an entire wall dedicated to surfer legends Brock Little, Kelly Slater and Derek Ho. Serves primarily American fare. Open for lunch and dinner. Reservations suggested.

Hula Grill Ka'anapali. *Moderate.* At the Whalers Village, 2435 Ka'anapali Pkwy., Bldg. P, Ka'anapali; (808) 667-6636/*www.hula-grill.com.* Beach front restaurant, housed in a 1930s-style Hawaiian beach house, and also featuring a "barefoot bar," in the sand. Serves Hawaiian regional cuisine prepared with fresh island ingredients. Menu includes grilled Hawaiian fish, crab cakes, steak, roasted chicken, and stir-fry vegetables in fiery Chinese black bean sauce. Open for lunch and dinner.

Jameson's Grill and Bar. *Moderate-Expensive.* 200 Kapalua Dr., Kapalua; (808) 669-5653. Country club setting, at the 18th hole at the Kapalua Bay Golf Course, with sweeping views of Molokai, Lanai and the ocean. Serves fresh island fish, seafood, lamb and steak; Aloha pie for dessert. Award-winning wine list. Open for breakfast, lunch and dinner.

Kimo's Restaurant. *Moderate.* 845 Front St., Lahaina; (808) 661-4811/*www.kimosmaui.com.* Landmark Lahaina restaurant in oceanfront setting, with panoramic views of Molokai and Lanai. Old Lahaina decor. Serves primarily fresh Hawaiian fish, seafood and prime rib; also Polynesian-style chicken. Lighter menu with cocktails on lower deck. Open for lunch and dinner. Reservations suggested.

Kobe Japanese Steak House. *Expensive.* 136 Dickenson St., Lahaina; (808) 667-5555. Authentic Japanese cuisine, including Teppanyaki-style steak and seafood, prepared at the table side. Also sushi bar. Open for dinner daily. Reservations recommended.

Lahaina Coolers. *Inexpensive-Moderate.* 180 Dickenson St.,

Lahaina; (808) 661-7082. Hawaiian-style French bistro, with a unique bar, made from an 11-foot longboard. Features tropical pizzas, and a good selection of pasta dishes and salads. Open for breakfast, lunch and dinner daily.

Leilani's on the Beach. *Inexpensive-Moderate.* In the Whaler's Village, Building J, 2435 Ka'anapali Pkwy., Ka'anapali; (808) 661-4495/*www.leilanis.com.* Open-air restaurant, situated on Ka'anapali Beach, with unobstructed views of the ocean. Offers fresh fish and seafood, as well as lamb, steak, chicken and prime rib; salads. Lunch menu features salads, sandwiches and burgers. Open for lunch and dinner. Reservations suggested.

Longhi's Restaurant. *Moderate-Expensive.* 888 Front St., Lahaina; (808) 667-2288. Traditional Italian cooking, featuring a variety of pasta dishes, veal, fresh fish, and steaks. Entertainment and dancing on weekends. Open for breakfast, lunch and dinner daily.

Moose McGillycuddy's. *Inexpensive-Moderate.* 844 Front St., Lahaina; (808) 667-7758. Popular local restaurant, featuring standard American fare, including chicken, steak, prime rib and seafood. Live entertainment. Open for breakfast, lunch and dinner daily.

Nalu Sunset Bar and Sushi. *Moderate.* At the Maui Marriott, 100 Nohea Kai Dr., Ka'anapali; (808) 667-1200. Fresh island fish and seafood; also salads. Open for lunch and dinner.

Ohana Bar & Grill. *Moderate.* At the Embassy Suites Resort, 104 Ka'anapali Shores Pl., Ka'anapali; (808) 661-2000. Casual pool side restaurant, overlooking the ocean. Features American cuisine primarily. Also fresh seafood, pasta and prime rib. Extensive wine list. Entertainment. Open for lunch and dinner daily.

Ono Bar & Grill. *Moderate.* At the Westin Maui, 2365 Ka'anapali Pkwy., (808) 667-2525/*www.westinmaui.com.* Hawaiian-style dinners, featuring seafood, salads, chicken and ribs; also burgers and thin crust pizza, and breakfast buffets. Pool side setting. Open for breakfast, lunch and dinner.

Pavillion. *Moderate.* Hyatt Regency Maui, Ka'anapali; (808) 667-4727/*www.maui.hyatt.com.* Pool side dining; casual atmosphere. Serves primarily American cuisine. Also breakfast buffet daily. Open for breakfast and lunch.

Pioneer Inn Grill & Bar. *Moderate-Expensive.* 658 Wharf St., Lahaina; (808) 661-3636. Housed in the Pioneer Inn; overlooking Lahaina Harbor. Serves primarily American fare. Informal setting. Open for breakfast, lunch and dinner daily.

The Plantation House Restaurant. *Expensive.* 2000 Plantation Club Dr., Lahaina; (808) 669-6299/*www.theplantationhouse.com.* Situated on the Plantation Golf Course at Kapalua, with views of Molokai and Lanai and the north shore of Maui; elegant setting. Menu features fresh island fish, and chicken, steak, filet mignon, duck breast and Australian lamb; also some vegetarian dishes and creative salads. Open for breakfast, lunch and dinner. Reservations recommended.

Royal Ocean Terrace Restaurant. *Inexpensive-Moderate.* At the Royal Lahaina Resort, 2780 Keka'a Dr., Ka'anapali; (808) 662-3210/(800) 280-8155/www.2maui.com. Standard American fare. Also breakfast buffets and Sunday brunch. Open for breakfast, lunch and dinner. Reservations suggested.

Roy's Kahana Bar and Grill. *Moderate-Expensive.* 4405 Honoapi'ilani Hwy., Kahana; (808) 669-6999/www.roysrestaurant.com. "Hawaiian Fusion Cuisine," blending local island ingredients with Asian spices and garnishes and European-flavor sauces. Menu features blackened island ahi, hibachi-style grilled salmon, mahi mahi, ribs, potstickers and shrimp. Also hot chocalate souffle. Open for dinner daily.

The Sea House Restaurant. *Moderate.* At the Napili Kai Beach Club, 5900 Honoapi'ilani Rd., Napili: (808) 669-1500. Delightful setting, overlooking Napili Bay. Specialties here are rack of lamb and fresh island seafood. Live Hawaiian entertainment, and dancing. Breakfast, lunch and dinner daily. Reservations recommended.

Tropica. *Expensive.* At The Westin Maui, 2365 Ka'anapali Pkwy., Ka'anapali; (808) 667-2525/www.westinmaui.com. Pacific Rim cuisine, served in delightful, oceanfront setting, amid tiki torches and tumbling falls. Menu features fresh island fish and flame-grilled steaks. Also fruit-flavored tropical desserts. Open for dinner. Reservations recommended.

Sansei Seafood Restaurant and Sushi Bar. *Moderate-Expensive.* 115 Bay Dr., Ste. 115, Kapalua; (808) 669-6286/www.sanseihawaii.com. Award-winning restaurant, offering sushi and Japanese-cum-Hawaiian cuisine, with emphasis on fresh island ingredients. Menu features shrimp tempura, vlobster, teriyaki beef, noodles, salads and vegetarian dishes. Open for dinner daily. Reservations suggested.

Smokehouse. *Moderate-Expensive.* 1307 Front St., Lahaina; (808) 667-7005. Offers a good selection of smoked and charcoal broiled ribs, steaks, seafood and chicken. Open for lunch and dinner daily.

Spat's Trattoria. *Moderate-Expensive.* At the Hyatt Regency Maui, Atrium Tower, 200 Nohea Kai Dr., Ka'anapali; (808) 667-4727/www.maui.hyatt.com. Traditional Northern Italian, served in cozy, intimate atmosphere. Menu includes shrimp and lobster filled ravioli, Milanese osso bucco and herb grilled filettini. Dancing after 10 p.m. Open for dinner daily. Reservations recommended.

Swan Court. *Expensive-Deluxe.* At the Hyatt Regency Maui, 200 Nohea Kai Dr., Ka'anapali; (808) 667-4727/www.maui.hyatt.com. Oceanfront setting, surrounded by waterfalls and a swan pond; acknowledged as one of the ten most romantic restaurants in the world. Offers gourmet cuisine; entrees include rack of lamb, pork tenderloin, lemongrass chicken, lobster and filet mignon. Also

SOUTHWEST COAST | Kihei

freshly-made, hot souffles. Open for dinner Tues., Thurs., and Sat. Reservations recommended.

The Terrace. *Expensive.* At the Ritz-Carlton Resort, One Ritz-Carlton Dr., Kapalua; (808) 669-6200. Features Pacific Rim cuisine, and seafood buffets on Fridays. Live Hawaiian entertainment. Open for dinner. Reservations recommended.

Thai Chef Restaurant. *Inexpensive.* Old Lahaina Shopping Center, Lahaina; (808) 667-2814. Authentic Thai food, with a complete vegetarian menu. Open for lunch Mon.-Fri., dinner daily.

Tiki Terrace. *Moderate.* At the Ka'anapali Beach Hotel, Ka'anapali; (808) 661-0011. Garden restaurant, serving Continental and Hawaiian cuisine, with emphasis on fresh seafood, chicken and beef. Hawaiian entertainment, including hula dancers. Open for dinner daily. Reservations recommended.

Va Bene Italian Beachside Grill. *Moderate-Expensive.* At the Maui Marriott, 100 Nohea Kai Dr., Ka'anapali; (808) 667-1200. Menu features Italian entrees prepared with local island ingredients. Specialties include lamb chops roasted with rosemary, filet mignon seared with port wine and balsamic demi-glace, and tiger prawns baked with asparagus. Also sumptious breakfast buffets. Open for breakfast, lunch and dinner, and brunch on Sundays. Reservations suggested.

SOUTHWEST COAST | 2

Kihei | Wailea | Makena

Kihei | 5   See Map 5 for Orientation

Northernmost on East Maui's southwest coast, some 19 miles southwestward from Lahaina (or 7 miles south of Kahului), is Kihei, historically important as a landing for Hawaiian war canoes, and with its associations to British explorer, Captain George Vancouver. Vancouver first landed here in 1792, and returned the following year, in 1793, bringing with him live cattle and root vegetables, which he introduced to Maui. There is a monument commemorating Vancouver's first landing here, located on the ocean side of South Kihei Road, directly across from Maui Lu Hotel.

Kihei, it must be fair to say, has no real town center as such; South Kihei Road runs directly north-south through the town, beginning at the intersection of Mokulele Highway (350) and Pi'ilani Highway (31), and continuing south toward Wailea. On one side of it—the ocean side—stand the hotels and a haphazard jumble of condominiums, and on the *mauka*—inland—side, shopping cen-

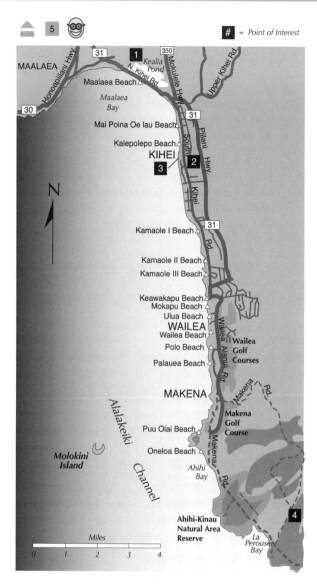

= Point of Interest

MAALAEA

Honoapiilani Hwy

31

350

1 Kealia Pond

N. Kihei Rd.

Mokulele Hwy

Upper Kihei Rd.

30

Maalaea Beach △

Maalaea Bay

31

Mai Poina Oe Iau Beach △

Piilani Hwy

South

Kalepolepo Beach △

KIHEI

2

3

Kihei

31

N

Kamaole I Beach △

Rd

Kamaole II Beach △

Kamaole III Beach △

Keawakapu Beach △
Mokapu Beach △
Ulua Beach △

WAILEA
Wailea Beach △

Wailea Alanui Rd.

Wailea Golf Courses

Polo Beach △

Palauea Beach △

MAKENA

Makena Rd.

Alalakeiki

Makena Golf Course

Puu Olai Beach △

Oneloa Beach △

Channel

Molokini Island

Ahihi Bay

Makena Rd.

Ahihi-Kinau Natural Area Reserve

4

La Perouse Bay

Miles

0   1   2   3   4

KIHEI, WAILEA AND MAKENA

1. Kealia Pond Bird Sanctuary
2. David Malo's Kiolani Church
3. Koieie Fishpond
4. Site of 1790 Lava Flow

SOUTHWEST COAST | Kihei

ters. This is not to say, however, that Kihei is without visitor interest. On the contrary, it has some six miles of sandy beaches, with views of West Maui and the nearby islands of Lanai, Kaho'olawe and **Molokini**—a partially-submerged, crescent-shaped crater, rising 150 feet from the ocean, and now a protected marine reserve and seabird sanctuary, quite popular with scuba divers and snorkeling enthusiasts, located just offshore, to the southwest.

Prominent among Kihei's beaches, situated just to the north of Kihei, off North Kihei Road (Highway 31), is Ma'alaea Beach, all of 3 miles long, with several access points, ideal for beachcombing and jogging, especially in the mornings; and across from there, on the *mauka* side of the highway, is the **Kealia Pond Bird Sanctuary**, a 300-acre wildlife refuge, where you can see, among others species of birds, Hawaiian stilts and coots, both indigenous waterfowl.

Among other beaches in Kihei are Maipoina Oe lau, a narrow roadside beach, and a good place for whale watching during the winter months, situated just off South Kihei Road, a half mile south of the intersection of Mokulele Highway; and Kalepolepo Beach, another half mile south on South Kihei Road, with some swimming possibilities. This last, Kalepolepo Beach, is also the site of the ancient **Ko'ie'ie Fishpond**, where you can still see the fishpond walls intact.

Another place of interest here, quite close to the Maipoina Oe lau and Kalepolepo beaches and also the Vancouver Monument, located a half mile or so on Kulanihakoi Road, is the Trinity Church by the Sea, originally the site of Hawaiian scholar **David Malo's Kilolani Church**, where Malo once preached outdoors. The church was reorganized in 1976, and, in keeping with tradition, services are still held there, outdoors.

South still, 4 or 5 miles, are the Kama'ole I, Kama'ole II and Kama'ole III beaches, with restrooms, showers and picnic tables, and good swimming possibilities—except during heavy surf or kona storms. Kama'ole I Beach, the northernmost of the three, also offers excellent bodysurfing possibilities near its north end, along a section of the beach known as Young's Beach; while Kama'ole III Beach features a playground area, especially good for families with children.

Wailea

   See Map 5 for Orientation

South from Kihei, approximately 2 miles, lies Wailea, a well-planned, exclusive resort community, fronting on a lovely, 2-mile-long white-sand beach, and reached on either the well-traveled South Kihei Road—which eventually becomes Wailea Alanui—or by way of the by-pass route, Pi'ilani Highway (31). In any case, Wailea has five world-class, luxury hotels—Marriott, Renaissance,

Four Seasons, Fairmont and the Grand Wailea Resort—several plush condominiums, and an excellent shopping center, the Wailea Shopping Village. It also has three championship, 18-hole golf courses, notable among them the Blue Course, site of the LPGA Women's Kemper Open, held in February every year; and scores of tennis courts, including those at the Wailea Tennis Club, billed as "Wimbledon West."

Among Wailea's hotels, the **Renaissance Wailea Resort** is perhaps most notable, originally built in 1978 as the Westin, then purchased in 1983 by Stouffer Hotels and upgraded a few years later, in 1987, at a cost of $7 million, and purchased and upgraded yet again, in the late 1990s, by Renaissance Hotels. The low-rise, 347-room hotel now boasts, besides its ocean view rooms with lanais, beautifully landscaped gardens, waterfalls, pool, whirlpool spas, 3 restaurants, an art-decorated lobby, and golf and tennis facilities. Additionally, the beach at the Renaissance offers some of the best swimming, snorkeling, windsurfing and sunbathing opportunities.

Wailea's other notable resort hotel is the 600-room **Maui Marriott**, originally built in 1976 as the Maui Inter-Continental Hotel, with the distinction of being the first hotel to be developed at Wailea. The hotel consists of one 7-story and 6 low-rise buildings, three swimming pools, golf and tennis facilities, and four full-service restaurants. The hotel also offers its very own helicopter tours of the island.

Wailea has some excellent sandy beaches as well—Keawakapu, Mokapu, Ulua, Wailea and Polo—which are, in fact, part of the 2-mile strip bordering the resort development. The beaches here are less crowded than the ones farther north at Kihei, and offer some of the best swimming, snorkeling and bodysurfing on the island. The Wailea beaches are also remarkably easily accessible, with well-marked access roads dashing off Wailea's main street, Wailea Alanui, to lead to them.

Makena

  5   *See Map 5 for Orientation*

South from Wailea, Wailea Alanui road becomes Makena Alanui and leads directly to Makena, a little over 2 miles distant. Makena is less developed than either Wailea or Kihei, with *kiawe* trees lining its beaches rather than resort developments, and with wild sorts of roads, largely unmarked, leading down to the beaches. However, Makena does have one or two good hotels and condominiums, notable among them the **Maui Prince Hotel**, a luxury hotel developed in 1986, offering 300 oceanfront guest rooms—with views of the islands of Lanai, Kaho'olawe and Molokini—three well-appointed restaurants, two swimming pools, and golf and tennis facilities. The hotel also features a delightful Japanese water garden with fish ponds, smaller rock gardens, waterfalls and small pagodas.

Makena also has some good sandy beaches that are well worth exploring. The Oneloa Beach, for one, commonly known as **Makena Beach** or "Big Beach," is perhaps one of the area's loveliest—an idyllic, white-sand beach, a half mile long, reached by way of Makena Alanui, some 3 miles south from the intersection of Kaukahi Road in Wailea, then off on a dirt road, heading *makai* (inland), another quarter mile or so to the beach. Interestingly, in the early 1970s nearly a hundred people—primarily hippies in search of an alternative lifestyle—inhabited the beach.

Adjoining to the north of Makena Beach and separated by the 360-foot-high cinder cone, Pu'u Olai, is Pu'u Olai Beach, also known as Little Beach. A trail leads over the rocky outcropping from Makena—or Big—Beach to Little Beach, the latter a lovely, crescent-shaped beach with excellent swimming and bodysurfing possibilities, as well as some promising snorkeling, on calm days, around Pu'u Olai Point. Little Beach, by the way, is also quite popular with nudists, although—a word of caution—Hawaii's state laws prohibit nude bathing at public beaches.

South still, another mile or two on Makena Road—which is really a continuation of Makena Alanui—lies the Ahihi-Kina'u Natural Area Reserve, a 2,045-acre preserve that includes in it an 807-acre undersea ecological reserve, originally established in 1979. Ahihi-Kina'u is also the site of the last **lava flow** on the island, which occurred in 1790, making this a rather barren tract of land, covered with a hard lava crust. The park, however, is a good place for snorkeling and scuba diving, especially when the ocean is calm.

Also of interest, one and one-half miles south of Ahihi-Kina'u, at the end of Makena Road, is La Perouse Bay, named for French nobleman and navigator, Compte de la Perouse, the first European to land on Maui, in 1786. La Perouse Bay is at once beautiful and desolate, popular, primarily, with fishermen and divers. From La Perouse Bay, too, the historic Hoapili Trail—or "King's Highway"—heads out east, passing by, near the bay itself, the ruins of an ancient fishing village. The trail begins roughly three-quarters of a mile from the end of the paved Makena Road—with a large white sign, standing in the midst of the hardened lava, indicating the trailhead—and journeys some 2 miles through the lava flow area to the secluded, rocky Kanaio Beach, more or less at the southern tip of the island.

Accommodations | Kihei, Wailea and Makena

Castle Kamaole Sands. *$195-$305*. 2695 S. Kihei Rd., Kihei; (808) 874-8700/(800) 367-5004/*www.castleresorts.com*. 345 condominium units, with TV, phones, air-conditioning, and kitchens. Swimming pool, tennis court and restaurant on premises. Daily maid service. Limited wheel-chair access.

The Fairmont Kea Lani Maui. *$595-$2,200*. 4100 Wailea Alanui, Wailea; (808)875-4100/(800) 882-4100/*www.kealani.com*. 450 rooms and suites in luxury beach front hotel. TV, phones, stereos, and kitchenettes. Swimming pool, health club and spa, restaurants, cocktail lounge, meeting rooms, shops and beauty salon.

Four Seasons Resort Wailea. *$365-$1,500*. 3900 Wailea Alanui, Wailea; (808) 874-8000/(800) 334-MAUI/*www.fourseasons.com*. 380-room luxury resort, overlooking Wailea Beach. Facilities include a swimming pool, health club with spa, tennis courts, restaurants and cocktail lounge, meeting rooms, and shops.

Grand Wailea Resort, Hotel & Spa. *$485-$2,000*. 3850 Wailea Alanui, Wailea; (808) 875-1234/(800) 223-6800/(800) 888-6100/*www.grandwailea.com*. Luxury, ocean-front resort hotel, with 787 rooms and suites. Hotel facilities include swimming pools, health club and spa, tennis courts, golf course, restaurants, shops and beauty salon. Handicapped facilities.

Hale Pau Hana Resort. *$175-$400*. 2480 S. Kihei Rd., Kihei: (808) 879-2715/(800) 367-6036/*www.hphresort.com*. 80 ocean-front condominium units, with TV, phones, and kitchens. Swimming pool. Handicapped facilities. Minimum stay: 5 days.

Kamaole Beach Royale Resort. $90-$180. 2385 S. Kihei Rd., Kihei; (808) 879-3131/(800) 421-3661/*www.mauikbr.com*. 65 condominium units with TV, phones and kitchens. Swimming pool, meeting rooms. Maid service. Handicapped facilities. Located directly across from beach. Minimum stay: 5 days.

Kihei Bay Vista. *$105-$125*. 679 S. Kihei Rd., Kihei; (808) 879-8866/(877) 971-2700/*www.kiheibayvista.com*. 60 condominium units; TV, phones, air-conditioning, kitchens. Swimming pool on premises. Daily maid service. Minimum stay, 2 days.

Kihei Beach Resort. *$160-$205*. 36 S. Kihei Rd., Kihei; (808) 879-2744/(800) 367-6034/*www.kiheibeachresorts.com*. 34 beach front condominium units, with TV, phones and air-conditioning. Swimming pool. Maid service. Handicapped facilities. Minimum stay: 3 days.

Kihei Kai. *$100-$140*. 61 N. Kihei Rd., Kihei; (808) 891-0780/(888) 778-7717/*www.kiheirentals.com*. 24 condominium units, with TV, air-conditioning, and kitchens. Swimming pool. Minimum stay: 4 days.

Kihei Surfside Condominium. *$140-$305*. 2936 S. Kihei Rd.,

Kihei; (808) 879-1488/(800) 367-5240/*www.kiheisurfsidei.com*. 83-unit oceanfront condominium complex. TV, phones, full kitchens; also swimming pool. Handicapped facilities. Minimum stay, 3 days.

Lihi Kai Cottages. *$120-$150.* 2121 Ili'ili Rd., Kihei; (808) 879-2335/*www.lihikai.com*. 9 oceanfront cottages, with kitchens, and TV. Maid service. Handicapped facilities. Minimum stay, 3 days.

Luana Kai Resort. *$99-$269.* 940 S. Kihei Rd., Kihei; (808) 879-1268/(800) 669-1127/*www.luanakai.com*. 113 units in oceanfront condominium complex; TV, phones, kitchens. Swimming pool, health club and spa, tennis court. Handicapped facilities. Minimum stay, 3 days.

Maui Makena Surf. *$455-$785.* 3750 Wailea Alanui Dr., Wailea; (808) 879-1595/(800) 367-5246/*drhmaui.com*. 25 oceanfront condominium units, with TV, phones, air-conditioning, and kitchens. Swimming pool, golf course, restaurant and cocktail lounge, shops. Maid service. Minimum stay: 3 days.

Mana Kai Maui Resort. *$100-$220.* 2960 S. Kihei Rd., Kihei; (808) 879-1561/(800) 367-5242/*www.crhmaui.com*. Beach front resort with 98 units with TV and phones; also some kitchen units. Swimming pool, restaurant and cocktail lounge, meeting rooms, shops and beauty salon. Maid service. Handicapped facilities.

Maui Coast Hotel. *$140-$270.* 2259 S. Kihei Rd., Kihei; (808) 874-MAUI/(800) 895-MAUI/*www.mauicoasthotel.com*. 261-room oceanfront hotel; TV, phones, air-conditioning. Swimming pool, tennis courts, restaurant and cocktail lounge, meeting rooms, and shops on premises. Handicapped facilities.

Maui Hill. *$150-$525.* 2881 S. Kihei Rd., Kihei; (808) 879-6321/(800) 922-7866/*www.astonhotels.com*. 42 condominium units, with TV, phones, air-conditioning, and kitchens. Swimming pool, tennis court. Maid service. Handicapped facilities.

Wailea Marriott Resort. *$269-$1,425.* 3700 Wailea Alanui Dr., Wailea; (808) 879-1922/(800) 367-2960/*www.marriott.com*. Oceanfront, luxury resort hotel, with 516 rooms and suites. Facilities include swimming pools, tennis courts, golf course, restaurant and cocktail lounge, meeting rooms, shops and beauty salon. Handicapped facilities.

Maui Lu Resort. *$110-$225.* 575 S. Kihei Rd., Kihei; (808) 879-5881/(800) 922-7866/(800) 321-2558/*www.astonhotel.com*. Beach front resort with 160 units with TV, phones, and air-conditioning. Swimming pool, tennis court, restaurant and cocktail lounge and shop on premises. Maid service.

Maui Prince Hotel. *$335-$1,500.* 5400 Makena Alanui, Makena; (808) 874-1111/(866) PRINCE-6/*www.mauiprince.com*. 310-room full-service hotel, fronting on the ocean. Hotel facilities include a swimming pool, tennis courts, golf course, restaurants, cocktail lounge, and meeting rooms. Handicapped facilities.

Maui Schooner Resort. *$195-$295.* 980 S. Kihei Rd., Kihei;

(808) 879-5247/(800) 877-7976/*www.mauischooner.com*. 47 units in oceanfront resort. TV, phones, and kitchens; also swimming pool, jacuzzi, spa, tennis courts, and putting greens. Handicapped facilities.

Maui Vista. *105-$170.* 2191 S. Kihei Rd., Kihei; (808) 879-7966/(800) 922-7866/(800) 321-2558/*www.resortquestmaui.com*. 279 condominium units, with TV, phones, air-conditioning, and kitchens. Also swimming pool and tennis court on premises. Maid service.

Nani Kai Hale. *$125-$215.* 73 N. Kihei Rd., Kihei; (808) 879-9120/(800) 367-6032/*www.nanikaihale.com*. Beach front condominium complex with 30 units with TV, phones and kitchens. Swimming pool. Maid service. Handicapped facilities. Minimum stay: 3 days.

The Palms at Wailea. *$170-$330.* 3200 Wailea Alanui, Wailea; (808) 879-5800/(888) 294-7731/(800) 367-7040/*www.outrigger. com*. 150 1- and 2-bedroom condominium units; TV, phones, air-conditioning, and kitchens. Swimming pool and health club and spa. Maid service. Handicapped facilities.

Maui Polo Beach Club. *$360-$570.* 3750 Wailea Alanui Dr., Wailea; (808) 879-1595/879-8847/(800) 367-5246/*www.drhmaui. com*. Oceanfront condominium complex, with 30 units with TV, phones, kitchens, air-conditioning, and maid service. Swimming pool, golf course, tennis court. Restaurant and cocktail lounge, meeting rooms, shops. Minimum stay: 3 days.

Shores of Maui. *$90-$225.* 2075 S. Kihei Rd., Kihei; (808) 879-6700/(800) 367-8002/(800) 888-6284/*www.leisurepropertiesinc. net*. 50 oceanfront condominium units, with TV and air-conditioning. Swimming pool. Minimum stay: 3 days.

Renaissance Wailea Beach Resort. *$300-$595.* 3550 Wailea Alanui, Wailea; (808) 879-4900/(800) 9-WAILEA/*www.marriott.com*. 347-unit luxury resort hotel, situated on the beach. TV, phones; swimming pool, tennis court, restaurant and cocktail lounge, meeting rooms, shops and beauty salon. Handicapped facilities.

Wailea Ekahi Village. *$200-$450.* 3750 Wailea Alanui Dr., Wailea; (800) 879-9272/(800) 367-2954/*www.drhmaui.com*. 295 oceanfront condominium units, with TV, phones, and kitchens; also swimming pool, tennis court, golf course, restaurant and cocktail lounge, and shops. Daily maid service. Minimum stay, 5 days.

Wailea Ekolu Village. *$175-$295.* 3750 Wailea Alanui Dr., Wailea; (808) 879-1595/(800) 367-5246/*www.drhmaui.com*. 30-unit condominium complex, situated on the golf course. TV, phones, kitchens; ocean views. Swimming pool, tennis court, golf facilities, restaurant and cocktail lounge, and shops. Maid service. Minimum stay, 3 days.

Wailea Elua Village. *$260-$780.* 3750 Wailea Alanui Dr., Wailea; (808) 879-1595/(800) 367-5246/*www.drhmaui.com*. 50

oceanfront condominium units, with TV, phones, and kitchens. Also swimming pool, tennis court, golf course, restaurant and cocktail lounge, and shops. Daily maid service. Minimum stay, 3 days.

Wailea Grand Champions. *$185-$410.* 3750 Wailea Alanui Dr.. Wailea; (808) 879-1595/(800) 367-5246/*www.drhmaui.com*. 25-unit condominium complex, situated on the Wailea Blue Golf Course. TV, phones, air-conditioning; swimming pool, tennis court and golf facilities. Restaurant and cocktail lounge. Daily maid service. Minimum stay: 3 days.

Dining | Kihei, Wailea and Makena

Cafe Kiowai. *Inexpensive-Moderate.* At the Maui Prince Hotel, 5400 Makena Alanui, Makena; (808) 874-1111/*www.princeresort-shawaii.com*. Open-air setting, casual atmosphere; overlooking garden and koi ponds. Offers Continental cuisine, featuring fresh seafood, prime rib, pasta and burgers, including a "Taro Burger"; also breakfast buffet. Open for breakfast and lunch daily. Reservations suggested.

Canton Chef. *Moderate.* Kamaole Shopping Center, Kihei; (808) 879-1988. Chinese cuisine, emphasizing seasonal, fresh food, prepared with a variety of spices. Open for lunch and dinner. Reservations suggested.

Dina's Sandwich. *Inexpensive-Moderate.* 145 N. Kihei Rd., Kihei; (808) 879-3262. Homemade soups, potato salad and other salads; also gourmet sandwiches. Full bar. Open daily.

Five Ponds Restaurant. *Moderate.* At Mana Kai Maui Hotel, 2960 S. Kihei Rd., Kihei; (808) 879-2607. Open-air setting; outstanding ocean views. Serves fresh Hawaiian fish and seafood; also beef, poultry, duck, prime rib and rack of lamb. Open for breakfast, lunch and dinner daily. Reservations suggested.

Ferraro's Bar and Ristorante. *Moderate-Expensive.* At the Four Seasons Resort, 3900 Wailea Alanui, Wailea; (808) 874-8000. Open-air restaurant in beachfront setting. Fresh island fish, seafood, and pasta dishes; pizzas baked in kiawe wood-burning oven for lunch. Open for lunch and dinner daily. Reservations suggested for dinner.

Hakone. *Expensive.* At the Maui Prince Hotel. 5400 Makena Alanui, Makena; (808) 874-1111/*www.princeresortshawaii.com*. Authentic Japanese cuisine, prepared in a variety of styles. Also sushi bar. Open for dinner daily. Reservations recommended.

Hula Moons. *Moderate-Expensive.* At the Wailea Marriott Resort, 3700 Wailea Alanui, Wailea; (808) 879-1922/*www.waileamarriott*.

com. Oceanfront restaurant with authentic Hawaiian ambience. Offers Hawaiian cuisine, with emphasis on fresh island seafood. Extensive salad bar. Live entertainment. Open for breakfast and dinner daily; also brunch. Reservations suggested.

Humuhumunukunukuapua'a. *Expensive.* At the Grand Wailea Resort, 3850 Wailea Alanui Dr., Wailea; (808) 875-1234/*www. grandwailea.com*. Authentic thatched-roof restaurant, situated beside lagoon. Serves primarily Hawaiian cuisine, with emphasis on fresh local seafood. Open for dinner daily. Reservations recommended.

Kaikuono. *Moderate.* 2511 S. Kihei Rd., Kihei; (808) 879-1954. Casual, ocean view setting, with views of the islands of Lanai, Kaho'olawe and Molokini. Offers seafood, steak, salads, burgers. Open for lunch and dinner daily.

Kihei Caffe. *Inexpensive-Moderate.* 1945 S. Kihei Rd., Kihei; (808) 879-2230. Casual eatery, offering local "kine" food, including burgers and island fish. Open for breakfast and lunch daily.

Kumu Bar and Grill. *Moderate.* At the Wailea Marriott Resort, 3700 Wailea Alanui, Wailea; (808) 879-1922/*www.waileamarriott. com*. Ocean view restaurant, offering Continental dishes; also buffets. Hawaiian entertainment nightly. Open for lunch and dinner. Reservations suggested.

Maui Onion. *Moderate.* At the Renaissance Wailea Beach Resort, 3550 Wailea Alanui, Wailea; (808) 879-4900/*www.renaissancehotels.com*. Informal, pool side setting. House specialties are Maui onion rings and tropical fruit smoothies. Open for lunch daily.

Outback Steak house. *Moderate.* Pi'ikea Shopping Center, off Pi'ilani Hwy., Kihei; (808) 879-8400. Casual setting with Australian outback theme. House specialties include fresh island fish, rack of lamb, steak and prime rib. Open for dinner daily.

Pacific Grill. *Moderate.* At the Four Seasons Resort, 3900 Wailea Alanui, Wailea; (808) 874-8000. Open-air restaurant, specializing in Pacific Rim fusion cuisine, combing flavors from East and West. Menu highlights steak and seafood. Lavish buffets. Breakfast, lunch and dinner daily. Reservations recommended.

Palm Court. *Moderate.* At the Renaissance Wailea Beach Resort, 3550 Wailea Alanui Dr., Wailea; (808) 879-4900. Overlooking lush tropical gardens; open-air setting. Features champagne breakfast buffets, and also dinner buffets. Open for breakfast and dinner daily.

Prince Court. *Deluxe.* At the Maui Prince Hotel, 5400 Makena Alanui. Makena; (808) 874-1111. Elegant, ocean view restaurant, serving Continental cuisine. Menu emphasizes island-inspired dishes. Extensive wine list. Entertainment. Open for dinner. Reservations recommended.

The Seawatch Restaurant. *Expensive.* 100 Wailea Golf Club Dr., Wailea; (808) 875-8080/*www.seawatchrestaurant.com*. Ocean view restaurant, with stunning views of Molokini and Kaho'olawe.

Offers innovative "coastal cuisine," with emphasis on fresh island fish, and Asian dishes; also steak, rack of lamb, duck and chicken preparations. Open for breakfast, lunch and dinner. Reservations recommended.

Spago. *Expensive.* At the Four Seasons Resort, 3900 Wailea Alanui, Wailea; (808) 874-8000. Elegant, well-regarded restaurant, owned and operated by celebrity chef Wolfgang Puck. Features Hawaii fusion cuisine, combining flavors of California and the Pacific Rim, with emphasis on fresh island fish and locally-grown organic products. Wine list showcases Californian, Australian, European and Chilean wines. Open for dinner daily. Reservations recommended.

Stella Blues Café. *Moderate.* Azeka Mauka on Pi'ikea Rd., Kihei; (808) 874-3779. Home-style cooking, featuring vegetarian and egg dishes, as well as lamb, ribs and shrimp. Late night bar. Open for breakfast, lunch and dinner.

CENTRAL MAUI | 3

Kahului | Pu'unene | Wailuku | Iao Valley State Park | Waikapu Valley

Kahului | *Kanaha Pond, Kanaha Beach, Sugar Museum* 6 *See Map 6 for Orientation*

Kahului, together with the adjoining city of Wailuku, is the commercial center of Maui, with most of the island's shops, shopping centers, restaurants and other facilities located there, mostly concentrated on Ka'ahumanu Avenue, the city's main street, which runs directly east-west and northeast-southwest through the heart of the city. Kahului, importantly, is also Maui's only deep-water port, from where all of the island's sugar and pineapple are shipped and where most of the freighters and cruise ships bound for Maui arrive, docking in the Kahului Harbor. Besides which, Maui's main airport, the Kahului Airport, is situated just to the east of the city, at the end of Keolani Place, a little over 2 miles from the center of town.

For visitors, Kahului has one or two places of interest, chief
 among them the **Kanaha Pond State Wildlife Sanctuary**, located off Hana Highway (36), near the intersection of Haleakala Highway (396), just to the east of the city center, and where you can see indigenous Hawaiian stilts and Hawaiian coots and other endangered species; and the **Kanaha Beach County Park**, located just off Alahao Street, which goes off Ka'a Street, which, in turn, goes off Keolani Place (Highway 380), northeastward. This last, the Kanaha Beach County Park, bordered by ironwoods and protected by a coral reef, has good picnicking and swimming possibilities, especially for children, and is quite popular with windsurfers of all ages and abilities as well.

UP 6

■ = Point of Interest

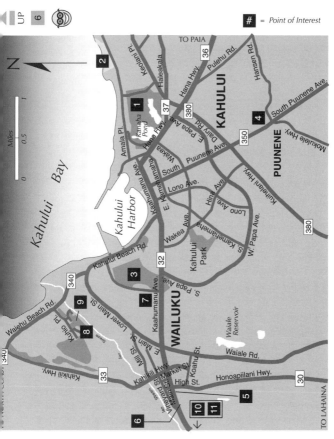

KAHULUI AND WAILUKU

1. Kanaha Pond State Wildlife Sanctuary
2. Kanaha Beach Park
3. Maui Zoological & Botanical Gardens
4. Alexander & Baldwin Sugar Museum
5. Kaahumanu Church
6. Hale Hoikeike (Bailey Museum)
7. Wailuku War Memorial Park
8. Pihana Heiau
9. Halekii Heiau
10. Kepaniwai Heritage Gardens
11. Iao Valley State Park

South from Kahului, on Pu'unene Avenue (Highway 350), a mile or so, lies Pu'unene, a satellite community of Kahului, which has in it, located at the corner of Pu'unene Avenue and Hansen Road, the **Alexander & Baldwin Sugar Museum**. Here you can see several sugar industry-related artifacts as well as scale models of the sugar factory, and also learn about sugar production—from the planting and harvesting of sugarcane, to the processing and bagging of refined sugar. The museum also has on display portraits of members of the Alexander and Baldwin families, together with family histories, as well as old photographs of men, women and children who

CENTRAL MAUI | Wailuku

worked in the company's factory and sugarcane fields. The museum itself is housed in the former home of the factory superintendent, surrounded by sugarcane fields, and directly across the street from there stands the Hawaiian Commercial & Sugar Mill, formerly the Alexander & Baldwin sugar mill, which is still in operation.

Wailuku

Ka'ahumanu Church, Hale Hoikeike, Maui Zoo

6   *See Map 6 for Orientation*

Adjoining to the west of Kahului is Wailuku, the seat of Maui County (which includes not only the island of Maui, but also Molokai, Lanai and Kaho'olawe). Wailuku is an historic town, with several old, historic buildings still there, mostly concentrated in its designated Historical District, on High, Market and Vineyard streets. Here, for instance, at the corner of High and Main streets, directly across from the Wailuku Courthouse, you can search out the New England-style **Ka'ahumanu Church**, built in 1837 and named for Queen Ka'ahumanu, one of the wives of King Kamehameha I. Queen Ka'ahumanu was an important convert to Christianity, who helped bring the religion into acceptance on Maui. The church now offers Hawaiian services—in Hawaiian!—on Sundays.

Close at hand, too, just west of the Ka'ahumanu Church, and also on Main Street, is **Hale Hoikeike**—"House of Display"—built between 1833 and 1850. Hale Hoikeike is notable as the former home of New England missionary Edward Bailey, who arrived in Maui in 1840, together with his wife, to teach at the Wailuku Female Seminary that was established here in 1833. The house is now a museum, and home to the Maui Historical Society. It houses displays centered around Hawaiian and missionary history, as well as a collection of Reverend Bailey's art, depicting scenes from the 1800s.

Also of interest, located on Market Street, near the corner of Main Street, is the Iao Theater, built in 1927 and used, over the years, alternately as a movie theater and playhouse. There are other buildings of historic note here as well, scattered throughout the historical district, which can be toured quite at random.

Also in Wailuku, a quarter mile north on Kanaloa Avenue—which goes off Ka'ahumanu Avenue—and directly across from the **Wailuku War Memorial Park**, are the **Maui Zoological and Botanical Gardens**. The zoo has some exotic birds, including peacocks, and monkeys, goats and other such animals; and the botanical gardens feature a small display of indigenous Hawaiian flowers and plants.

Iao Valley

Kepaniwai Park, Iao Valley State Park, Iao Needle

Westward from Wailuku lies the lush Iao Valley, reached more or less directly on Main Street and Iao Valley Road, along a rather scenic drive, with mountains rising on either side of the road. But before reaching the valley, a half-mile or so from the Wailuku township, and also of interest, are the Tropical Gardens of Maui, where you can see several plants and trees indigenous to the Hawaiian islands. There is a snack bar and gift shop at the gardens.

From the Tropical Gardens, it is another mile or so to the **Kepaniwai Park**, located in the valley, which has in it sections of art and architecture depicting the ethnic and cultural diversity of the island. Here you can see a typical Hawaiian grass hut, a Japanese pagoda surrounded by Japanese gardens and sculpture, a Portuguese villa, a New England salt-box, and Chinese, Filipino and Korean dwellings. The park also offers good picnicking and walking possibilities.

Ironically, Kepaniwai has a tragic past. In 1790, when King Kamehameha I invaded Maui in his bid to subjugate and unite all the Hawaiian islands under his reign, it was the scene of a bloody massacre. Kamehameha, it is told, landed his war canoes in Kahului, then drove the island's defenders back into Iao Valley, where they were mercilessly slaughtered. There were, in fact, so many islanders killed that their bodies filled the Iao Stream; hence the name, Kepaniwai, meaning, "damming of the waters."

Another half mile west of Kepaniwai on Iao Valley Road, there is a turnout, from where you can see what many will tell you is the naturally-sculpted profile of John F. Kennedy. The profile can be discerned on a black rock deep in the gorge. There is also a viewfinder here, on the side of the road, to help you locate and focus on the profile.

Farther still, another quarter mile from the John F. Kennedy profile, at the end of Iao Valley Road, lies the **Iao Valley State Park**, a 4-acre park that has at the center of it, as its chief attraction, the **Iao Needle**—a moss-covered stone spire that rises some 1,200 feet vertically from the valley floor (or 2,250 feet above sea level). There is also a trail that loops through the park, offering visitors abundant opportunities to view the Iao Needle and explore the surrounding area, criss-crossed by streams and dotted with natural pools and guava trees and wild, yellow ginger plants. The valley itself extends farther back toward the West Maui Mountains, to the extinct volcano, Pu'u Kukui, which rises to 5,788 feet, the highest point in West Maui. Pu'u Kukui also has the distinction of being one of the wettest spots on earth, with an average annual rainfall of over 400 inches!

Maui Tropical Plantation

From Wailuku, too, 3 miles south on Honoapi'ilani Highway (30), you can visit **Maui's Tropical Plantation**, situated on a 120-acre estate in the Waikapu Valley. The plantation is of course one of Maui's foremost tourist attractions, and a showcase of Hawaii's bounty of fruits and nuts. Here, a tram whisks visitors through groves of mango, guava, papaya, banana and macadamia nut trees, and sections of coffee and flowers such as orchids and hibiscus, and pineapple and sugarcane fields. There is also a restaurant at the plantation, the Tropical Restaurant, which features all-you-can-eat tropical luncheon buffets; and the Made-on-Maui Marketplace, where you can buy fresh, locally-grown Valley Isle produce.

Accommodations | Kahului

Maui Beach Hotel. *$105-$550.* 170 Ka'ahumanu Ave., Kahului; (808) 877-0051/(888) 649-3222/(800) 367-5004/(800) 272-5275/ *www.elleairmaui.com* or *www.castleresorts.com*. 142 units, with TV, phones and air-conditioning. Swimming pool, restaurant and cocktail lounge, meeting rooms, shops and beauty salon. Handicapped facilities.

Maui Seaside Hotel. *$125-$150.* 100 West Ka'ahumanu Ave., Kahului; (808) 877-3311/(800) 560-5552/*www.mauiseasidehotel. com*. 192 units; TV, phones, air-conditioning. Swimming pool, restaurant and lounge.

Dining | Kahului and Wailuku

Ichibana. *Moderate.* 47 Ka'ahumanu Ave., Kahului; (808) 871-6977. Japanese, American and Hawaiian fare, with sushi bar open for lunch and dinner. Specialties include shrimp tempura, teriyaki chicken and oxtail soup; also daily specials. Open for breakfast, lunch and dinner, Mon.-Sat.

Mama's Fish House. *Expensive.* 799 Poho Pl., Kuau; (808) 579-8488/*www.mamasfishhouse.com*. Popular Maui restaurant with authentic island decor, situated on the beach at Kuau Cove, just east of Paia; also offers outdoor dining. Menu features fresh Hawaiian seafood, including lobster and shrimp, and kalua duck as well as beef preparations. Open for lunch and dinner. Reservations recommended.

Marco's Grill and Deli. *Moderate.* 395 Dairy Rd., Kahului; (808) 877-4446. Authentic Italian cuisine, with a wide selection of pasta dishes and salads; also vegetarian preparations, seafood, grilled Italian sandwiches., cold sandwiches, burgers, and pizza. Open for breakfast, lunch and dinner daily.

Saeng's Thai Cuisine. *Moderate.* 2119 Vineyard St., Wailuku; (808) 244-1567. Good selection of Thai food, including appetizers, soups and salads. Entrees include seafood specialties, and curried chicken, beef and pork, prepared in a variety of styles; also several vegetarian dishes. Open for lunch Mon.-Fri., and dinner daily. Reservations suggested.

Tropical Restaurant. *Moderate.* At the Maui Tropical Plantation, on Honoapi'ilani Hwy., Waikapu; (808) 244-7643. A favorite with visitors to Maui. Offers tropical buffets and locally-grown fruit and nuts. Hawaiian country entertainment. Open for breakfast, lunch and dinner daily. Reservations recommended.

UPCOUNTRY | 4

Pukalani | Makawao | Kula | Ulupalakua Ranch | Haleakala National Park

Upcountry, quite broadly, comprises the western slopes of Mt. Haleakala. It is a lovely area, characteristic in its green pasture lands, dotted quite randomly with cattle, and its fertile soil where the bulk of Maui's fruit, vegetables and flowers are grown. Upcountry also enjoys significantly lower temperatures, typically 5°-15° cooler than the coastal areas of the island. Besides which, there are several good vista points here, many with commanding, unobstructed views of West Maui and the Kihei-Wailea coast.

South to Makawao   *See Map 7 for Orientation*

There are two routes by which to reach Upcountry from Central Maui. The first of these sets out directly from Kahului along Haleakala Highway (37), some 8 miles south to the town of Pukalani, the first town reached in Upcountry. Pukalani means "hole in the clouds," a name which, locals will tell you, is derived from the fact that the town always seems to have the sun shining on it, with clouds rarely lingering overhead. Pukalani itself has very little to interest the visitor, but is a good base from which to explore the Haleakala National Park.

An alternate route to Upcountry is by way of Paia—located just to the east of Kahului on Hana Highway (36)—from where Baldwin Avenue (Highway 390) heads directly south, approximately 7 miles, to Makawao in the Upcountry. This latter route has some added attractions. Just a mile from the center of Paia, for instance, on

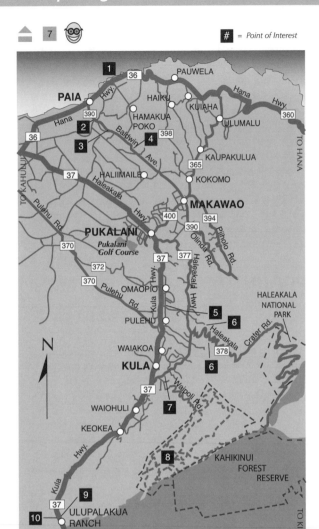

= Point of Interest

UPCOUNTRY

1. Hookipa Beach
2. Paia Sugar Mill
3. Holy Rosary Church
4. Baldwin Memorial Home
5. Maui Enchanting Gardens
6. Sunrise Protea Farm
7. Kula Botanical Gardens
8. Polipoli Springs State Recreation Area
9. Tedeschi Vineyards
10. Makee Sugar Mill
11. Site of Maui's last eruption (1790)

Baldwin Avenue, is the historic **Paia Sugar Mill**, the oldest continuously operating sugar mill on Maui, originally built around the turn of the century; and south of there, another mile or so, is the beautiful, red-brick **Holy Rosary Church**, where there is a statue of Father Damien, noted for his humanitarian work in the once-dreaded leper colony on the nearby island of Molokai. Also of interest, quite close at hand, is the Makawao Union Church, built in 1869 and featuring a lovely stained-glass window.

Yet another place of interest for the visitor to the area, a mile or so south of the Union Church on the highway, is the **Baldwin Memorial Home**, formerly the home of plantation owners Henry and Ethel Baldwin, built in 1917. The home now houses the **Hui Noeau Visual Arts Center**, which features a variety of art shows and workshops, and classes on ceramics, landscape painting, jewelry making, and the like.

Makawao

   See Map 7 for Orientation

Another one and one-half miles on Highway 390 and we are at Makawao—in Upcountry. Makawao is an old Hawaiian cowboy town that still boasts a few real *paniolos*—Hawaiian cowboys—who often ride into town on horseback for their supplies. The town also hosts what has become the biggest rodeo in the state of Hawaii, held on the Fourth of July every year, at the Oskie Rice Arena on Olinda Road (Highway 390), roughly a mile south of town. The rodeo showcases a variety of Western events, as well as a parade through town.

Makawao is a town that is best explored on foot, with its wood-frame buildings with false fronts reminiscent of the Old West, now filled with shops and restaurants, interspersed, quite strangely, with yoga centers and herbalists, offering a unique contrast between two very different worlds.

From Makawao, a worthwhile detour is Olinda, journeying south on Olinda Road, just past the Oskie Rice Arena, along a 9-mile loop that leads through groves of eucalyptus and pine trees, to finally emerge on Pi'iholo Road—Highway 394—at the very bottom, then northward again, back to Makawao.

From Makawao you can follow Highway 365, some 2 miles, directly west to Pukalani, then south on the all-important Haleakala Highway to Kula, the Haleakala National Park, and Ulupalakua Ranch and the Tedeschi Vineyards.

Kula

7   *See Map 7 for Orientation*

Protea Farms

Kula is situated at an elevation of 3,000 feet, approximately 6 miles south of Pukalani, reached by way of either Kula Highway (37) or Haleakala Highway (377). It is an area rich in agriculture, producing the bulk of Maui's vegetables, including such staples as Maui red onions, potatoes, lettuce and tomatoes. In fact, a little over a century ago, at the start of the historic California Gold Rush, the Kula country even supplied California with a substantial portion of its potato needs, earning for itself the name, "Nu Kalifornia."

Kula is also abundant in flowers. Most of the carnations used in leis throughout Hawaii are grown here. Besides which, the area is home to the exotic protea, originally brought to Hawaii from Australia and South Africa. The proteas flourish on Kula's mountain slopes, and are among Hawaii's most beautiful flowers, to be found in a variety of shapes, sizes and colors. A good place to see and buy proteas is the Sunrise Market on Haleakala Highway (377), adjacent to the Kula Lodge. Or you can visit the **Sunrise Market & Protea Farm** farther along on Highway 378 (which goes off 377), where you can also tour the protea gardens.

Also on Haleakala Highway, near the intersection of Kula Highway (37), are the **Kula Botanical Gardens**, where you can see a variety of plants and flowers—including protea, orchids and several types of ginger—as well as native kukui and koa trees, the latter especially prized for their wood, used in handcrafted Hawaiian furniture and wooden bowls.

Of interest, too, south from Kula, some 5 miles, is the **Polipoli Springs State Recreation Area**, situated on the southwestern slopes of Haleakala, at an elevation of around 6,200 feet, and reached on the mountainous Waipoli Road—partly unpaved—which goes off southeast from Haleakala Highway, a half-mile or so north of the intersection of the Kula (37) and Haleakala highways. The park itself is quite lovely, largely forested, with groves of pine, cypress, eucalyptus and towering redwoods. The park also has several miles of wooded hiking trails, as well as camping facilities.

Ulupalakua Ranch and Tedeschi Vineyards

Also south from Kula on Kula Highway is Keokea, a small town with one or two stores and a well-liked local eatery; and roughly six miles south of there lies the Ulupalakua Ranch, a 20,000-acre working ranch with approximately 500 cattle, 1,000 sheep and 40 elk. In the late 1800s, the ranch was owned by pioneer James Ma-kee, who planted much of the acreage to sugarcane; but following Makee's death, the new owners transformed Ulupalakua into the present-day ranch.

At the Ulupalakua Ranch, of interest to the visitor, are the **Tedeschi Vineyards**, Hawaii's only winery, located more or less at the center of the ranch along Kula Highway. The winery is owned and operated by former Napa Valley vintners, Emil and Jo Ann Tedeschi, who arrived here in 1973 and began experimenting with grape varieties, and found the Carnelian grape to be best suited to the Upcountry soil and climate. The Tedeschis now offer four differ-ent grape wines, including two sparkling wines, and—you guessed it—a pineapple wine. There is also a tasting room at the winery, housed in a century-old jailhouse. Of interest, too, directly across the street from the winery, are the ruins of the old **Makee Sugar Mill**, originally built in 1878.

10

11

South from the Ulupalakua Ranch, Kula Highway becomes Pi'ilani Highway (31) and journeys along a desolate section of the island—skirting the southwest corner of Haleakala—toward Hana, offering, enroute, some spectacular views of Kaho'olawe Island and Molokini, which lie just offshore. The highway also passes over a section of lava flow from Haleakala—the **last eruption on Maui**—which occurred in 1790. The lava flow, in fact, extends all the way south to La Perouse Bay and the Ahihi-Kina'u Natural Area Reserve.

12

Some 19 miles from the Tedeschi Winery the paved road ends, and not until another 7 miles or so farther, at Kipahulu, does it re-sume. However, the unpaved section of the highway is not entirely impassable, especially in dry weather conditions, and it has on it, at an approximate midway point—some one and one-half miles along—the tiny village of Kaupo, inhabited by only a handful of *paniolos* (Hawaiian cowboys). At Kaupo, too, a dirt road dashes off toward the ocean, to the picturesque Huialoha Church, situated on a wind-swept peninsula, dating from 1859. Also at Kaupo, you can search out the small, quaint Kaupo Store, decorated with antique cameras and other vintage photographic equipment, as well as a handful of *heiaus*: the Hale O Kane Heiau, Popoiwi Heiau and Lo'alo'a Heiau, the last of these dating from the 16th century.

Six miles farther, and we are at Kipahulu, where the paved high-way begins again, continuing northeastward toward Hana.

UPCOUNTRY | Haleakala

Haleakala National Park 8   See Map 8 for Orientation

No tour of Maui would be complete without a visit to the spectacular Mt. Haleakala—"House of the Sun"—the world's largest dormant volcano, situated in the 30,183-acre Haleakala National Park in the southeast part of the island. The park can be reached from Kahului on Highways 36 and 37 (Haleakala Highway) southeastward to Pukalani; from Pukalani it is another 6 miles or so on Highway 377 to the Haleakala Crater Road (Highway 378) which journeys more or less directly eastward along a steep, winding route, some 12 miles, to the park. Alternatively, if you are already at Kula, take Highway 377 northeastward roughly 3 miles, then east on Highway 378 and so to the Haleakala park. From the park entrance, it is another 10 miles south on Haleakala Crater Road, climbing some 3,200 feet or so, to the summit, **Pu'u Ulaula**—"Red Hill." The route passes by the **Leieiwi** and **Kalahaku overlooks**, at elevations of 8,000 feet and 9,000 feet, respectively, with the latter boasting some silverswords—a rare flower stalk, 3-8 feet tall, with pointed, silvery leaves, that blooms only once before dying and is indigenous to Haleakala—growing in an enclosure near it. From the summit at **Pu'u Ulaula**, at an elevation of 10,023 feet, you can gaze down into the mammoth crater—3,000 feet deep, 7½ miles long and 2½ miles wide—sweeping across a vast lunar landscape. From here, too, you can view the entire island of Maui, as well as the nearby islands of Molokai, Lanai, Kaho'olawe, and even Hawaii, the Big Island, to the south. There are two or three trails looping through the crater as well, including the Silversword Loop Trail which has some silverswords along it, and the Sliding Sands and Halemau'u trails that also journey through the crater. Besides which, there is a visitor center situated on the rim of the crater, quite close to the summit, with exhibits and information on the geology and eruption history of Haleakala.

Haleakala is one of Hawaii's great wonders, and among the tallest mountains in the world, with a base some 20,000 feet beneath the ocean, and its head more or less perpetually in the clouds, more than 10,000 feet above. It is also a place of immense beauty and mysticism, and a source of infinite, unharnessed energy. Indeed, novelist Jack London described it in his *House of the Sun* as "a noble dwelling situated on the island of Maui," with "a message of beauty and wonder for the human soul that cannot be delivered by proxy."

Haleakala, it must be fair to say, is also a place of spirituality, sacred to Hawaiians, where the *kahunas*—Hawaiian priests—once worshipped, and where, we are told, in times immemorable, demigod Maui, son of goddess Hina, lassoed the sun and forced it to slow its path over the great mountain in order that his mother

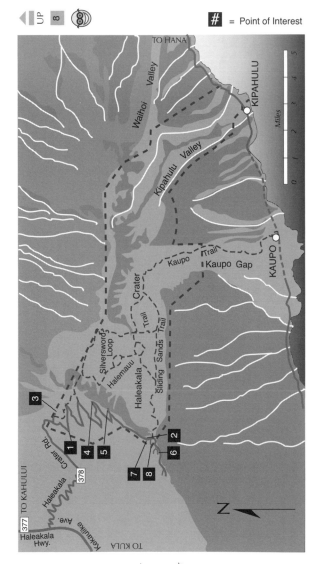

= Point of Interest

HALEAKALA NATIONAL PARK

1. Park Head-quarters
2. Visitor Center
3. Hosmer Grove
4. Leleiwi Overlook
5. Kalahaku Overlook
6. Science City
7. Puu Ulaula (Red Hill)
8. Red Hill Overlook

may dry her *kapa* cloth. According to legend, Maui braided a rope from coconut fiber, tied a noose at one end of it, and lay in wait for the sun in "The House of the Sun"; and as the sun journeyed over the mountain, Maui lassoed the sun's rays, one at a time, and broke them off, until the sun surrendered to him. And so, to this day, the sun lingers longer over Haleakala.

The best time to visit Haleakala is of course at sunrise, before the morning clouds smother the peak, although sunsets can be just as spectacular. It is advisable to dress warmly for the morning spectacle, as the temperatures are likely to be at least 30° below those in the island's lower elevations. It is also a good idea to get a weather report for Haleakala at 808-877-5111 before visiting.

Haleakala National Park, besides the Haleakala Crater, has one or two other points of interest as well. At the north end of the park is **Hosmer Grove**, which has a variety of trees, including pines, spruce, eucalyptus and firs, all planted in 1910 by Ralph Hosmer, regarded as "Hawaii's Father of Forestry," and for whom the grove is named. There is also a half-mile trail that loops through the grove, and a campground to boot.

Worth visiting, too, quite close to the Hosmer Grove, is the **Park Headquarters-Visitor Center**, which has maps, brochures and books on the park's geology, flora and fauna, and where you can also see, outside the center, some *nene*—or Hawaiian Goose— Hawaii's state bird. The *nene,* typically, live in the high country around Haleakala. Once close to extinction, they now have a stable population of around 150.

Finally, there is **Science City**, at the south end of the park, past the Haleakala summit, Pu'u Ulaula. Science City is essentially a University of Hawaii research facility—although part of the facility is also used by NASA—devoted to the research of solar and lunar activity. It is, however, generally not open to the public.

Accommodations | Upcountry: Kula

Bloom Cottage. *$135-$165.* Kula Hwy. (37), Kula; (808) 878-1425/(800) 398-6284/*www.ho'okipa.com.* 2-bedroom cottage, situated at an elevation of 3,000 feet, with superb views of West Maui, Lanai and Kaho'olawe. Laura Ashley-style furnishings; full kitchen. Complimentary juice and muffins.

Kula Lodge. *$120-$175.* Haleakala Hwy. (377), Kula; (808) 878-1535/(800) 233-1535/*www.kulalodge.com.* 5 chalet-style units with private lanais, overlooking Central and West Maui. Restaurant and lounge on premises.

Haikuleana Inn. *$110-$149.* 555 Haiku Rd., Haiku; (808) 575-7500/*www.haikuleana.com.* Historic, 1860s plantation home, located one and one-half miles from the beach. Features 4 antique-furnished guest rooms, with private baths. Full breakfast and fresh flowers daily in the rooms. A "very Hawaiian experience."

Dining | Upcountry: Makawao and Kula

Casanova Italian Restaurant & Deli. *Moderate.* 1188 Makawao Ave., Makawao; (808) 572-0220. Traditional, home-style Italian cooking, featuring lasagna, homemade pasta and seafood dishes; also salads, and pizzas baked in a wood-burning oven. Entertainment. Open for dinner. Reservations suggested.

Hali'imaile General Store. *Moderate-Expensive.* 900 Hali'imaile Rd., Hali'imaile; (808) 572-2666. Specializing in traditional American cuisine, including steak, prime ribs, lamb chops; also fish, and salads. Homemade desserts. Country store setting. Open for lunch Mon.-Fri., dinner daily.

Kula Lodge & Restaurant. *Moderate-Expensive.* Haleakala Hwy. (377), Kula; (808) 878-1535. Full-service restaurant, with superb views of Central and West Maui. Contemporary cuisine, prepared with fresh island ingredients; Menu features salads, lamb, filet mignon. Also flavorful macadamia nut pancakes for breakfast. Open daily for breakfast, lunch and dinner. Reservations suggested.

Makawao Steak House. *Moderate.* 3612 Baldwin Ave., Makawao; (808) 572-8711. Established Makawao restaurant, noted for its steaks and seafood. Casual atmosphere. Open for dinner.

Polli's Mexican Cantina. *Inexpensive-moderate.* 1202 Makawao Ave., Makawao; (808) 572-7808. Casual family restaurant, serving authentic Mexican food and drinks. Entertainment. Open for lunch and dinner daily.

HAWAIIAN FLOWERS

Hibiscus

Anthurium

Bird of Paradise

Torch Ginger

White Ginger

Plumeria

Passion Flower

Lobster Claw

Miss Joaquin Orchids

Silversword

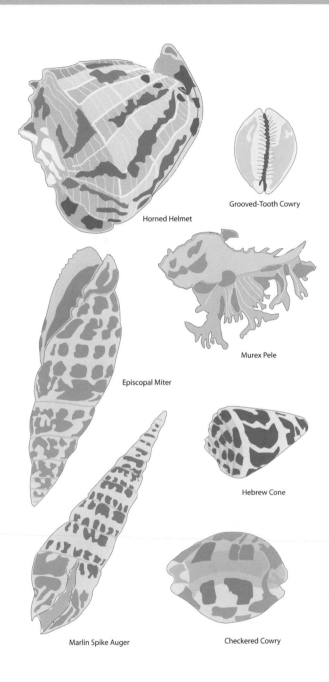

Horned Helmet

Grooved-Tooth Cowry

Murex Pele

Episcopal Miter

Hebrew Cone

Marlin Spike Auger

Checkered Cowry

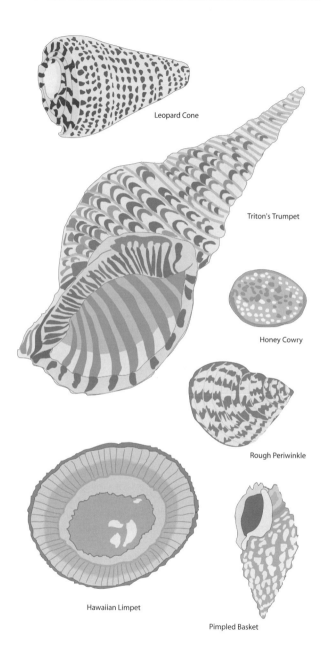

Leopard Cone

Triton's Trumpet

Honey Cowry

Rough Periwinkle

Hawaiian Limpet

Pimpled Basket

ROAD TO HANA | 5

Paia | Ho'okipa | Keanae Peninsula | Wailua | Hana

The Road to Hana—or the Hana Highway—is one of the most beautiful drives in the islands. It sets out from just outside Kahului and journeys southeast along the coast, some 55 miles, to the sleepy little town of Hana. The highway twists and turns madly much of the way—around 617 curves!—passing by lush, verdant valleys and scores of picturesque waterfalls, large and small, crossing some 56 tiny bridges, mostly one-lane. And while it is possible to drive to Hana in less than two hours, this is one drive that should be enjoyed, even experienced, at a leisurely pace, for it offers some of the most breathtaking ocean and valley views, almost at every turn of the highway, and abundant opportunities for taking dips in refreshing, cool, emerald pools beneath waterfalls—with picnicking beside them—and rare moments of solitude.

| **Paia** | *Ho.okipa Beach, H.P. Baldwin Beach Park, Paia Sugar Mill* | 9 | *See Map 9 for Orientation* |

At the top of the Hana Highway, some 6 miles east of Kahului, lies the small, quaint town of Paia, formerly a sugar plantation camp, established at the turn-of-the-century. The town is filled with an assortment of colorful little shops, boutiques and galleries, along with a handful of eateries, mostly dating from the late 1960s and early 1970s when Paia was a sleepy little village, inhabited primarily by hippies. Paia is now also famous for its windsurfing, with much of the activity centered on nearby **Ho'okipa Beach**—situated 2 miles or so from the center of town, and reached on the main highway, Hana Highway (36), eastward—where you can watch world-class windsurfers perform 360-degree flips in the waves and generally hone their skills. Ho'okipa Beach Park is also the site of the annual Hawaiian Pro, held in April, as well as several other national and international windsurfing competitions.

Just to the west of Paia, a half-mile or so off the highway, lies H.P. Baldwin Beach Park, with a long, sandy beach. The park is quite popular with bodysurfing enthusiasts, and was once also the site of Maui's first bodysurfing competition, held in 1977.

Paia has one or two other points of interest as well. Just to the east of town, also off the highway, stands the Mantokuji Buddhist Temple, with its ornate decorations and landscaped Japanese gardens, overlooking the ocean; and a little to the south of the center of town, about a mile on Baldwin Avenue—which goes off the

ROAD TO HANA | Paia

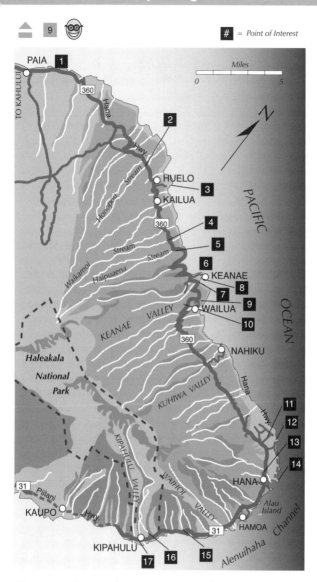

= Point of Interest

THE ROAD TO HANA

1. Hookipa Beach Park
2. Twin Falls
3. Kaulanapueo Church
4. Waikamoi Ridge Trail
5. Haipuaena Falls
6. Keanae Peninsula
7. Keanae Lookout
8. Ihiihi o lehowa o na Kaua Church
9. St. Gabriel's Church
10. Keanae Valley-Wailua Overlook
11. Kahanu Gardens
12. Waianapanapa State Park
13. Helani Gardens
14. Kauiki Head
15. Wailua Falls
16. Oheo Gulch
17. Palapala Hoomau Church and Lindbergh Grave

highway (36)—you can search out the old, historic Paia Sugar Mill, still in operation and with the distinction of being the oldest sugar mill in continuous operation in Maui. The mill was built around the turn-of-the-century by the Alexander & Baldwin interests, founders, too, of Paia.

Southeast from Paia

Twin Falls, Kaulanapueo Church, Waikamoi Ridge Trail, Haipua'ena Falls

Southeast from Paia, some 10 miles, Hana Highway 36 becomes Hana Highway 360 and the "Road to Hana" begins in earnest, with open, blue ocean on one side of it, and lush, green hills and valleys on the other. Approximately 2 miles from where Highway 360 begins, the road crosses over a highway bridge, the Ho'olawa Bridge, the first of several bridges on the Hana Highway, just to the west of which a well-worn trail dashes off inland a little way, alongside **2** a stream, to two successive waterfalls, appropriately named **Twin Falls**. The first of the two falls lies a mile or so from the highway, with a small pool at the foot of it, well worth stopping at for a dip; and the second, and larger, of the two falls can be reached by following the trail upstream from the little pool, another quarter mile, to a large, natural pool, more secluded than the first, into which the fuller, second waterfall plunges. And here, too, you can enjoy the pristine pool and picnic beside it.

From Twin Falls, it is another mile or so to the tiny village of Huelo, reached on a small side road, Huelo Road, which goes off the highway toward the ocean, and where you can search out the **3** old, stone-and-coral **Kaulanapueo Church**, dating from 1853 and situated on a cliff overlooking the ocean; and southeast from there, another 6 miles approximately, is an unmarked turnout at the head **4** of the **Waikamoi Ridge Trail**—a picturesque, mile-long nature trail that leads past a variety of indigenous plants and trees, including eucalyptus and a bamboo. The trail also offers magnificent views along the way, of the Waikamoi Valley and the coastline below, and good picnicking opportunities besides.

Farther still, another half mile—just before mile marker 10—are the Waikamoi Falls, located quite close to the road and easily accessible; and a mile or so southeastward from there, at mile marker 11, is the bridge over Puohokamoa Stream, from where a short trail dashes off back into the valley, to the picturesque, and more popular, Puohokamoa Falls, where there are some picnic tables and a fair-sized natural pool, ideal for swimming. Also worth investigat- **5** ing, a half mile from the Puohokamoa Falls, are the **Haipua'ena Falls**, more secluded than the Puohokamoa Falls, and also with a small, emerald pool at the foot of the waterfall. The Haipua'ena Falls can be reached by following a short trail overgrown with wild ginger, that goes off the highway from near the southern end of the one-lane highway bridge.

Another half mile from the Haipua'ena Falls, and we are at the Kaumahina State Wayside Park, which has a picnic area and restroom facilities, and an overlook with superb views of the Hono-manu Bay and the rugged coastline farther to the southeast. A little way from the park, too, journeying on the highway toward Hana, you can see, on the inland side, the ancient Honomanu Valley that has in it towering cliffs and a waterfall or two, but is largely inaccessible.

Ke'anae Peninsula

See Map 9 for Orientation

From Kaumahina State Wayside Park, it is another 4 miles or so to the beautiful Ke'anae Peninsula, a more or less flat tract of land, jutting out northward into the ocean. But first, before reaching the peninsula, situated alongside the highway itself—a half mile past mile marker 16—is the **Ke'anae Arboretum**, where you can view a variety of indigenous Hawaiian plants and trees, including native forest trees, tropical trees introduced to Hawaii, and cultivated Hawaiian plants. Also at the arboretum are irrigated patches of *taro*—from the root of which, *poi,* a Hawaiian staple rich in nutrients, is made—and an authentic representation of a Hawaiian rain forest.

In any event, **Ke'anae Peninsula**, quite picturesque with its green patchwork quilt of *taro,* and originally formed by a lava flow from the Haleakala Crater that passed through the Ko'olau Gap and the Ke'anae Valley on the way to the coast, can be reached on a side road that goes off Hana Highway, just past the Ke'anae Arboretum, northeastward. Ke'anae itself is rural and quite serene, with a handful of small homesteads set amid the *taro*. But it does have something to interest the visitor: the lovely, steepled **Lanakila 'ihi'ihi o lehowa o na Kaua Church**, built from stone and coral, dating from 1860. At Ke'anae, too, at the northern tip of the peninsula, you can visit Ke'anae Point, which has superb, commanding views of the ocean.

Also of interest, a half mile from the Ke'anae turnoff, just past mile marker 17, is the **Ke'anae Overlook**, unmarked, but with stunning, picture-postcard views of the Ke'anae Peninsula; and a little way from there, another half mile or so, is the halfway point to Hana, dotted with a handful of fruit-stands—best known among them the long-established Uncle Harry's—all located alongside the highway, and where you can sample a variety of locally-grown fruit—star fruit, papayas, mountain apples and strawberry guavas.

ROAD TO HANA | Wailua to Hana

Wailua to Hana

See Map 9
for Orientation

Wailua

Southeastward from the halfway mark to Hana, past mile marker 18, Wailua Road dashes off the highway toward the ocean, to the little village of Wailua, which has not one but two steepled churches—the stone-and-coral **St. Gabriel's Church**, where services are now held, and the adjacent, surprisingly small, historic Coral Miracle Church, built in 1860 from coral washed onto Wailua Beach, following a freak storm. There are also some good views from here, looking inland, of the scenic Waikani Falls, cascading more than a hundred feet.

A little farther on, just past mile marker 19, on the *mauka*—inland—side of the highway, is the **Ke'anae Valley-Wailua Lookout**, which offers spectacular views of the lush Ke'anae Valley that extends all the way to Ko'olau Gap, more or less to the rim of the Haleakala crater. At the lookout, too, following the stairs to the right, you can enjoy a splendid view of Wailua directly below.

Farther still is Pua'aka'a State Wayside Park, situated approximately midway between mile markers 22 and 23 on Hana Highway. The park has in it one or two small waterfalls, with a delightful little pool and a gushing spring, and some good picnicking possibilities. A short walk from the highway, on the *mauka* side, leads to the falls.

Kahanu Gardens and Wai'anapanapa State Park

Another 8 miles or so, at mile marker 31, Ulaino Road dashes off the highway, seaward, one and one-half miles, to Kalahu Point, where you can visit the beautiful **Kahanu Gardens**, a 126-acre tropical botanical garden that is now part of the National Tropical Botanical Garden. The garden grows and displays a collection of ethnobotanical plants—including breadfruit and coconut trees—which have been used by Hawaiians for centuries for their nutritional and medicinal properties, as well as in clothing, baskets and dishes. There is also a visitor's center here that has guidebooks for the garden, detailing a self-guided walking tour of the grounds.

Also at the Kahanu Gardens is Hawaii's largest *heiau*—or temple—the Pi'ilanihale Heiau, meaning "Home of Pi'ilani" (Pi'ilani was the first chief of Maui, during the 15th century). The *heiau* stands 50 feet tall, overlooking ancient fishponds. It is also one of the oldest such relics on the island, dating from 1270 A.D.

Next up, at mile marker 32, is **Wai'anapanapa State Park**, lying just two miles north of the town of Hana. Wai'anapanapa, meaning "glistening water," derives its name from a large lava-tube cave located in the park, reached by way of a well-marked trail that starts out at the northeast end of the parking area, and which has in it some natural pools with good swimming possibilities. The cave, interestingly, is also intertwined with a local legend, which endures that Maui's Chief, Ka'akea, once suspected his wife, Popoalaea, of infidelity, thus invoking his wrath. Popoalaea, needless to say, fled from her husband and hid in this cave, where, eventually, Ka'akea found and killed her. On certain nights, it is told, the pools in the cave turn a murky red from the blood of the slain Princess Popoalaea—a grim reminder of the infamous event. (In reality, though, it is the thousands of tiny red shrimp that fill the pools from time to time that give the water the bloody red tint.)

In any case, Wai'anapanapa State Park has a lovely picnic area, directly above a small, black-sand beach, as well as camping facilities and rental cabins. It also has, at the front of the picnic area, a natural rock arch, which adds to the interest. Swimming is not encouraged at the beach, due to the fact that the bay is largely unprotected, making it rather unsafe for the activity. From Wai'anapanapa, an old Hawaiian trail leads to Hana, journeying along the coastline for the most part, passing by growths of *hala*, ancient burial sites, and *heiaus*.

Also worth visiting, just out from Hana, roughly a mile past Wai'anapanapa State Park, are the **Helani Gardens**—a lovely, 70-acre, drive-through botanical garden, filled with lavish displays of Hawaiian plant life. The garden offers picnicking and walking possibilities.

From the Helani Gardens, it is another mile, approximately, south on Hana Highway to Hana, our main destination.

Hana

  See Map 10 for Orientation

Hana, frequently romanticized as "Heavenly Hana," and situated at the head of Hana Bay, at the eastern end of the island, is a surprising little town, rural, secluded, tranquil, unpretentious, and largely unchanged in more than a hundred years. It was originally founded as a sugar plantation town in 1864—one of the earliest on the island—where sugar remained the principal industry until the early 1930s, bringing to the area hundreds of Chinese, Japanese and Portuguese plantation workers, whose descendants—together with several full-blooded Hawaiians—continue to make up the major portion of Hana's resident population of around 1,000.

The town itself is really quite easy to explore, with only a half-dozen or so streets, all told. At the heart of it are the Hotel Hana-Maui and Hana Ranch, the latter established in the 1940s by

Paul Fagan, a San Francisco millionaire. In 1943, Fagan purchased some 14,000 acres of prime sugarcane land in and around Hana, following the collapse of the sugar industry, and converted the cane fields into ranch land. The Hana Ranch—which, along with the Hotel Hana-Maui, is the chief employer in the Hana area—is now a working ranch of sorts, encompassing some 4,500 acres on the outskirts of town, and where guests of the Hotel Hana-Maui can enjoy horseback and hay-wagon rides, among other outdoor pursuits. The ranch, however, is usually not open to the general public.

1 **Hotel Hana-Maui** is quite possibly *the* centerpiece of Hana, situated more or less at the center of town, just off Hana Highway, between Keawa Place and Hauoli Street. It was originally built in 1947, also by Paul Fagan, as the Hotel Hana Ranch, an exclusive resort for his well-heeled guests. The hotel itself, which boasts among its guests such celebrities as bestselling author James Michener and former Beatle George Harrison, consists of 12 rather simple, single-story bungalow-style buildings (housing 97 guest rooms and suites in all), with thatched roofs—luxury accommodations, no less!—tucked away among palms, fruit trees, ferns and other native plants and flowers, on a 23-acre site. The hotel also features an open lobby—also with a thatched roof—and two well-appointed restaurants—with hula shows featured at one of them on certain nights of the week—as well as a fresh-water swimming pool, tennis courts, and a small, 3-hole golf course. Besides which, there is a sandy beach just to the south of here, with excellent swimming and sunbathing possibilities, where the hotel staff organize activities and catered meals for guests, including traditional Hawaiian luaus.

Also of interest, directly across from Hotel Hana-Maui, on Lyon's **8** Hill, stands a large lava-stone cross, built as a **memorial** to Paul Fagan, following his death in 1959. From the top of the hill you can enjoy good views of the ocean and Hana Bay and the Hana township below.

Among other places worth visiting here, are the **Wananalua 5 Church**, dating from 1838 and built from coral blocks, located adjacent to Hotel Hana-Maui on the Hana Highway; the **Hana 6 Cultural Center**, located on Uakea Road, just to the north of Keawa Place, which has in it a small museum displaying various Hawaiian artifacts, such as quilts, bowls and historic photographs, and where you can also visit the old courthouse and jail cells; and the famous **7 Hasegawa Store**, quite possibly Hana's foremost tourist attraction, which burnt down in August, 1990, and was subsequently relocated at its present address, at 5165 Hana Highway. This last, the Hasegawa Store, is much to be recommended to visitors to Hana. It is an historic, family-run general store, piled high with almost every imaginable item—from groceries to lawn-mowers to stereo systems—and immortalized in song and visited, over the years, by a host of celebrities: Kris Kristofferson, Jim Nabors, Steve Forrest, Richard Pryor, Carol Burnett, Burt Reynolds and George Harrison, among others.

Try to also visit the glorious Hana Bay at the east end of town, along the southern shore of which, reached more or less directly on Keawa Place—which goes off Hana Highway, passing through the center of town—is **Hana Beach Park**, with a sandy beach with good swimming possibilities, and a popular little eatery, Tutu's. Just to the east of the beach, too, at the southeastern corner of Hana Bay rises **Kauiki Head**, a 386-foot-high, red cinder cone, site of several pitched battles for the defense of the island. At Kauiki Head, in fact, in 1780, Maui's King Kahekili successfully repelled an onslaught

= Point of Interest

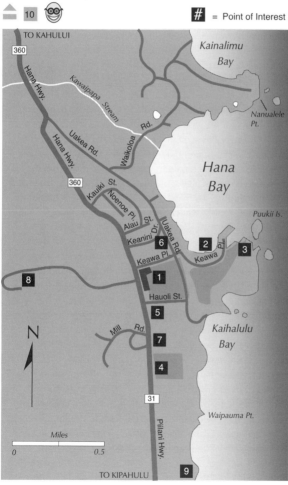

HANA

1. Hotel Hana Maui
2. Hana Beach Park
3. Kauiki Head
4. Hana Hongwanji Buddhist Temple
5. Wananalua Church
6. Hana Cultural Center
7. Hasegawa Store
8. Fagan Memorial Beach
9. Hamoa Beach

from Hawaii's King Kalaniopu'u, in one of the most famous battles fought on the island. Kauiki Head is also notable as the birthplace of Queen Ka'ahumanu, the favorite wife of King Kamehameha I, who was instrumental in breaking down the ancient Hawaiian *kapu* system by persuading Kamehameha II to eat a meal at the table with women.

South from Hana, Hana Highway becomes Pi'ilani Highway (31), and strung along it, just out from town, are two delightful beaches, Koki and Hamoa. The first of these, Koki Beach Park, located a little over a mile from town, along Haneo'o Road (which goes off the highway), is a popular surfing and bodysurfing beach, lined along its upper slope with ironwood trees, and from where you can also see, just offshore, Alau Island, a seabird sanctuary. The other, **9** **Hamoa Beach**—which is used by Hotel Hana-Maui guests, but is also a public beach—lies a mile or so to the south of Koki Beach, also off Haneo'o Road, and offers good swimming and bodysurfing possibilities as well.

South from Hana, too, Pi'ilani Highway narrows and becomes decidedly serpentine, weaving madly around hairpin bends and treating the motorist to some spectacular coastal scenery much of the way. Some 7 miles south of Hana, of course, at Wailua, you **9** **15** can view the picturesque, 95-foot **Wailua Falls**, and 3 miles farther, at the ocean end of the Kipahulu Valley—which comprises the southeastern corner of Haleakala National Park, with Paukea Stream **9** **16** meandering through the midst of it—lies the wild, lush **Oheo**—or "Seven Sacred Pools"—**Gulch**. The name, Oheo, however, is rather misleading, for the area has in it not seven but well over 20 natural pools—most with some swimming possibilities—and the pools, we are told, are in no way sacred. In any case, the gulch has a fair number of waterfalls as well, small and large, and a handful of scenic hiking trails, including a half-mile loop that leads to a series of lower pools, closer to, and overlooking, the ocean, and a 2-mile trail that journeys to the Waimoku Falls, farther back in the gulch, passing by the Makahiku Falls and crossing over one or two streams as it winds through some astonishing bamboo forests. Oheo Gulch also offers good views of the ocean and the Big Island of Hawaii to the south, and has in it a ranger station from where you can obtain weather and other information before venturing into the gulch.

From Oheo Gulch it is roughly a mile on Pi'ilani Highway to Kipahulu, a tiny village that has in it the historic Palapala Ho'omau Church, dating from 1857, and a small, seaside cemetery adjacent to the church where you can search out the grave of pioneer aviator **9** **17** **Charles A. Lindbergh**, buried here in 1974. Also near the church is the Kipahulu Point Park, comprising a small, grassy area, situated atop Kipahulu Point and overlooking the ocean. The park has good picnicking possibilities.

Beyond Kipahulu, a mile or so, the paved road ends, and not until 7½ miles farther, past the village of Kaupo, does it begin again.

Accommodations | Hana

Aloha Cottages. *$65-$95.* 73 Keawa Pl., Hana; (808) 248-8420. 5 rental accommodations, including a studio unit and 3-bedroom house; all units have kitchens, and some have phones.

Hana Bay Vacation Rentals. *$85-$17.* P.O. Box 318, Hana, HI 96713;(808) 248-7727/*www.hanahideaways.com*. 14 rental accommodations with TV and phones; some kitchens. Comfortable houses, in various locations in the Hana area.

Hana Kai - Maui Resort. *$125-$195.* 1533 Uakea Rd. (near Keanini Dr.), Hana; (808) 248-8426/(800) 346-2772/*www.hanakai. com*. 20 studio and one-bedroom units; all with kitchens and private lanais. Swimming pool.

Hana Accommodations and Plantation Houses. *$69-$150.* P.O. Box 489, Hana, HI 96713; (808) 248-7868/(800) 657-7723/(800) 228-4262/*www.hana-maui.com*. 12 rental accommodations, ranging from studio units to 2-bedroom cottages; all have TV, phones, and kitchens. Minimum stay: 2 days.

Heavenly-Hana Inn. $80-$90. Hana Hwy. (near Uakea Rd.), Hana; (808) 248-8442/*www.heavenlyhanainn.com*. 6 self-contained units, including 4 with Japanese decor. TV, kitchenettes, private lanais.

Hotel Hana-Maui. *$395 -$2,500.* 5031 Hana Hwy. (Cnr. Hana Hwy. and Keawa Pl.), Hana; (808) 248-8211/(800) 321-HANA/ *www.hotelhanamaui.com*. 96-room luxury hotel, with in-room phones. Hotel facilities include a swimming pool and spa, tennis court, 3-hole golf course, restaurants and cocktail lounge, meeting rooms, shops and beauty salon.

Dining | Paia and Hana

Cafe Mumbo. *Inexpensive.* Baldwin Ave., Paia; (808) 579-8021. Casual fare, including burger, salads, sandwiches. Open for breakfast, lunch and dinner daily.

Fresh Mint. *Inexpensive-Moderate.* 115 Baldwin Ave., Paia; (808) 579-9144. A wholly vegetarian, Vietnamese restaurant, offering a variety of Southeast Asian dishes. Casual atmosphere. Open for lunch and dinner daily.

Hana Ranch Restaurant. *Moderate.* At the Hotel Hana-Maui, Hana Hwy., Hana; (808) 248-8255/*www.hotelhanamaui.com*. Steaks and seafood on weekends; pizza on Wednesday nights. Also buffet-style lunch. Open for lunch daily, dinner Wed., Fri. and Sat. Reservations suggested.

Moana Bakery & Cafe. *Moderate.* 71 Baldwin Ave., Paia; (808) 579-9999/*www.moanacafe.com*. Full-service bakery and restaurant in casual setting. Offers local cuisine featuring fresh herbs and vegetables from the chef's own garden. Menu highlights fresh seafood, rack of lamb, beef, pasta and vegetarian dishes. Also good selection of classic French pastries and other homemade desserts, including fruit tarts, turnovers and eclairs. Live entertainment weekly. Open for brunch, lunch and dinner.

Tutu's at Hana Bay. *Inexpensive.* Keawa Pl., Hana; (808) 248-8224. Popular local eatery, located at the Hana Beach Park at Hana Bay. Offers sandwiches and burgers primarily. Open 8.30 a.m.-4 p.m. daily.

THINGS TO SEE AND DO

Places to See | Points of Interest at a Glance

West Maui

Baldwin Home. 120 Dickenson St. (Cnr. Front and Dickenson Sts.), Lahaina; (808) 661-3262/*www.lahainarestoration.org*. Former home of missionary-physician Reverend Dwight Baldwin, originally built in 1838, from coral, stone and timber, and now fully restored. The house is now a living museum, filled with original furnishings and several personal and household items of the Baldwin family, including old photographs. Open daily, 10-4; admission fee: $3.00 adults, $2.00 seniors, $5.00 family.

Banyan Tree. Located near the corner of Front and Hotel Sts. in Lahaina. This is one of the oldest and largest trees of its kind in the islands, planted in 1873, by Lahaina Sheriff W.O. Smith, to commemorate the 50th anniversary of the arrival of the missionaries in Lahaina. Originally from India, the Banyan Tree covers approximately an acre of land, with branches extending nearly 50 yards, supported by aerial roots that grow downward into the ground, and 12 major trunks.

Brig *Carthaginian II*. Anchored in the Lahaina Harbor, directly across from Pioneer Inn, in Lahaina; (808) 661-3262/*www.lahainarestoration.com*. Authentically restored, square-rigged brig; replica of the 19th-century ship that brought the first missionaries to the islands. Now houses a small museum below deck, with exhibits on whales and whaling, and also ongoing film on whaling. Museum hours: 10-4 daily. Admission fee: $3.00.

Hale Pa'ahao. Cnr. Prison and Waine'e Sts., Lahaina. Old stone jail (Hale Pa'ahao means "stuck in irons house"), built in 1854, from coral blocks taken from Lahaina's Old Fort at the Banyan Square. The jail has been largely preserved in its original state, much as it appeared in the 1850s, with one cell displaying a mannequin of an old salt, and another a list of convictions handed down in the 1860s and 1870s, as well as a diary of an inmate once confined to the cell. Open daily, 9-5. Free admission.

Hale Pai. Housed in the Lahainaluna Seminary, at the end of Lahainaluna Rd., just outside Lahaina. Hale Pai—meaning "house of printing"—is one of the oldest printing presses in the West, where the first Hawaiian-language newspaper was printed in 1834. It now houses a small museum, with displays of samples of some of the early type and printing, including some first editions of books printed here in the 1830s, and a replica of the original Ramage printing press. Open 10-4. Mon.-Fri.; donations accepted. (808) 661-3262/667-7040/*www.lahainarestoration.com*.

Jodo Mission. Located at 12 Ala Moana St. (which is a continuation of Front St.), approximately a mile north of downtown Lahaina; (808) 661-4304. Features one of the largest Buddha statues—cast in bronze—outside Asia, which was erected in 1968, to commemorate the centennial of the arrival of the first Japanese immigrants in Hawaii, in 1868. The mission park is open to the public daily during daylight hours.

Master's Reading Room. Cnr. Front and Dickenson Sts., Lahaina. Located adjacent to the Baldwin Home, this is one of the oldest structures in Maui, dating from 1833, and originally used as storage space by early missionaries, and later on as an officers' club for ship captains, masters and officers. Now restored, the Reading Room houses the offices of the Lahaina Restoration Foundation. Open during business hours.

Old Courthouse. Located on the harbor side of the Banyan Tree Square (near the Banyan Tree), in Lahaina. The old center of government activities, originally built in 1859, including in it a jail. The courthouse and jail now house two art galleries. Open during business hours.

Pioneer Inn. 658 Wharf St., cnr. Front and Hotel Sts., Lahaina; (808) 661-3636/*www.pioneerinnmaui.com*. Historic, 48-room inn, located adjacent to the Banyan Tree, overlooking Lahaina Harbor. The inn was originally built in 1901, and is reflective, in its architecture and decor, of Lahaina's whaling period, with antique whaling equipment and photographs of 19th-century whaling expeditions adorning its walls. Now houses two restaurants, a bar, and shops; also offers overnight accommodations.

Wailoa Church. Waine'e St., Lahaina. Formerly the Waine'e Church; originally built in 1823, and destroyed and rebuilt several times over the years, the last in 1988, when it was renamed "Wailoa." The church is significant in that Keopuolani, wife of Kamehameha I and mother of Kamehameha II and Kamehameha III, converted to Christianity here. There is also an ancient cemetery located adjacent to the church, the *Wailoa Cemetery,* where Hawaiian royalty and early missionaries are buried.

Whalers Village Museum. 2435 Ka'anapali Pkwy., Bldg. G-8, Ka'anapali; (808) 661-5992. Houses exhibits and artifacts centered around Maui's whaling era, including old photographs, charts, compasses, bone hooks, guns, spears and other weapons and tools used in whaling. Also displays depicting whale biology, with a description of how the different parts of a whale are used—including whale bone—and how oil is extracted from whale blubber. Open daily, 9 a.m.-10 p.m. Free admission.

Wo Hing Society Temple. Located on Front St., north from the center of town, in Lahaina. Historic Chinese temple, originally built in 1912 as a fraternal and social meeting hall for Hawaii's Chinese population. Now houses a museum, devoted to Chinese culture, with Chinese artifacts and exhibits, including a Taoist shrine. There is also a small, historic theater adjacent to the temple, the *Cookhouse Theatre,* which features some fascinating old films of Hawaii, shot by Thomas Edison in 1898. The theater and museum are open to the public daily 10-4. (808) 661-3262/*www.lahainarestoration. com.*

Central Maui

Alexander & Baldwin Sugar Museum. Cnr. Pu'unene Ave. (Hwy. 350) and Hansen Rd., Pu'unene (south of Kahului); (808) 871-8058/ *www.sugarmuseum.com.* 1,800 square foot museum, housing an extensive collection of artifacts depicting the history of Maui's sugar industry, including old photographs of sugar mill and sugarcane field workers, and portraits of members of the Alexander and Baldwin families. Also on display are scale models of the original Alexander & Baldwin sugar mill, and exhibits describing the sugar-making process—from the planting and harvesting of the sugarcane, to the processing and bagging of the sugar. Open 9.30-4.30, Mon.-Sat. Admission fee: $5.00 adults, $2.00 children.

Hale Hoikeike - Bailey House Museum. 2375-A Main St., Wailuku; (808) 244-3920/*www.mauimuseum.org.* Former home of New England missionary Edward Bailey, built between 1833 and 1850. Now houses a museum, devoted to Hawaiian and missionary history. Also features a collection of Reverend Bailey's art, depicting scenes from the early and mid-1800s. Open 10-4, Mon.-Sat. Admission fee: $5.00 adults, $1.00 children.

Ka'ahumanu Church. Cnr. Main and High Sts., Wailuku. Picturesque, New England-style church, dating from 1837 and named for Queen Ka'ahumanu, the favorite wife of King Kamehameha I, and one of Maui's first converts to Christianity. The church offers Hawaiian services on Sundays.

Kanaha Pond State Wildlife Sanctuary. Located off Hana Hwy. (36), near the intersection of Haleakala Hwy. (396), just east of

Kahului. Wildlife preserve, where Hawaiian stilts, Hawaiian coots, and other endangered species of such indigenous wildlife can be seen. There is also an observation shelter here, overlooking the pond and marshlands of the sanctuary.

Kepaniwai Heritage Gardens. Situated along Iao Valley Rd., approximately 2 miles west of Wailuku, in the Iao Valley. Scenic public park; features examples of art and architecture depicting the ethnic diversity of the island, including a typical Hawaiian grass hut, a Japanese pagoda surrounded by Japanese gardens and sculpture, a Portuguese villa, a New England salt-box, and Chinese, Filipino and Korean dwellings. The park also offers good picnicking possibilities. Open to the public daily.

Iao Valley State Park. Situated at the end of Iao Valley Rd., some 3 miles west of Wailuku. 4-acre park in delightful valley setting. The park has in it, more or less at the center of it, the picturesque Iao Needle, a 1,200-foot, moss-covered stone spire that has the distinction of being one of the most photographed sights in Maui. The park also has good hiking and picnicking possibilities.

Maui Nui Botanical Gardens. Located at 150 Kanaloa Ave., ¼ mile north of the intersection of Ka'ahumanu Ave. (directly across from the Wailuku War Memorial), in Kahului; (808) 249-2798/ *www.mnbg.org*. Display of indigenous Hawaiian plants and flowers, with emphasis on flora of Maui Nui (Maui, Molokai, Lanai and Kaho'olawe). Also center for environmental education, conservation, biological study, recreation, and Hawaiian cultural expression. Hosts several events throughout the year. Open 8-4, Mon.-Sat.

Maui Ocean Center. 192 Ma'alaea Road, Wailuku; (808) 270-7000/*www.mauioceancenter.com*. State-of-the-art aquatic center and marine park, developed at a cost of $20 million and opened to the public in 1998. "The Hawaiian Aquarium" houses an amazing collection of Hawaiian marine life, with live coral displays, showcasing sea turtles, sharks, rays, and hundreds of endemic animal species. Includes a unique acrylic tunnel through a 750,000-gallon "Open Ocean Exhibit" filled with more than 2,000 fish. Also outdoor touch pools and interactive displays. Open year-round, daily 9-5 (9-6 in July and August). Admission fee: $21.00 adults, $18.00 seniors, $14.00 children 3-12 (under 3 free).

Maui Tropical Plantation. Located on Honoapi'ilani Hwy. (30), between mile markers 2 and 3, just south of Wailuku. A 60-acre working plantation, this is one of Maui's foremost tourist attractions, where a tram whisks visitors through groves of mango, guava, papaya, banana and macadamia nut trees, sections of coffee and Hawaiian flowers, and pineapple and sugarcane fields. There is also a restaurant at the plantation, with all-you-can-eat tropical luncheon buffets, and a market offering fresh, locally-grown produce. Open 9-5 daily; free admission. Tour cost: $9.50 adults/$3.50 children. (800) 451-6805/*www.mauitropicalplantation.com*.

Tropical Gardens of Maui. Located at 200 Iao Valley Rd., ¼ mile west of Main St., in Wailuku: (808) 244-3085/*www.tropicalgarden-sofmaui.com*. Well-kept botanical gardens, featuring several species of native Hawaiian plants, as well as plants introduced to the Hawaiian islands. Open 9-5, Mon.-Sat.; admission fee: $3.00 adults.

Upcountry

Haleakala National Park. Situated 37 miles southeast of Kahului, more or less in the center of the island, and reached by way of Haleakala Hwy. (37) southeast from Kahului to Pukalani (7 miles), then Hwy. 377 directly south another 6 miles, from where Haleakala Crater Rd. (Hwy. 378) goes off eastward, 12 miles, to the park; (808) 572-4400/visitor center (808) 572-4461/weather hotline (808) 877-5111/*www.nps.gov/hale* (official site); or you can visit the unofficial site at *www.haleakala.national-park.com*. 30,183-acre park, which has in it the 10,023-foot Mt. Haleakala, the largest dormant volcano in the world, with a crater that is 3,000 feet deep, 7½ miles long and 2½ miles wide. Offers good hiking possibilities, including a trail that loops through the crater; also picnicking, camping and horseback riding. There is also a Visitors Center at the park, with exhibits and information on the geology and eruption history of Haleakala. Admission fee: $10.00 per car (7-day pass); bikers and hikers, $5.00 per person (7-day pass).

Hui Noeau Visual Arts Center. On Baldwin Ave. (Hwy. 390), between mile markers 5 and 6, Makawao; (808) 572-6560/*www.huinoeau.com*. Housed in the Baldwin Memorial Home, formerly the home of plantation owners Henry and Ethel Baldwin, dating from 1917. The arts center features a variety of art shows, workshops, and classes on ceramics, landscape painting and jewelry making. Permanent and changing exhibits. Gift shop on premises. Gallery hours: 10-4, daily.

Kula Botanical Gardens. Kekaulike Rd. (377), Kula; (808) 878-1715. 6-acre garden in natural setting, with a variety of Hawaiian and exotic plants and flowers—including several types of proteas, orchids and ginger—as well as native kukui and koa trees. Stream, carp pond, bird sanctuary and picnic area; also gift shop on premises. Open 9-4 daily; admission: $5.00 adults, $1.00 children.

Maui Enchanting Gardens. Kula Hwy. (37), Kula; (808) 878-2531. 8-acre botanical garden, featuring lush tropical plants and a variety of native fruit trees. Gift shop on premises. Hours: 9-5 daily. Admission fee: $5.00 adults, $1.00 children.

Polipoli Springs State Recreation Area. Located approximately 5 miles south of Kula, at the end of Waipoli Rd. (which goes off Kekaulike Ave., 377, a half mile north of Kula Hwy., 37,). Densely forested park, situated on the slopes of Mt. Haleakala at an elevation of 6,200 feet. Offers several miles of well-marked hiking trails,

MAUI | Points of Interest

winding through groves of pine, cypress, eucalyptus and redwood; also camping possibilities. Open daily.

Sunrise Market & Protea Farm. 416-A Hwy. 378, Kula; (808) 878-1600. Protea gardens open to the public for self-guided walks. Also open for retail sales, with more than 30 varieties of the flower available. Additionally, Sunrise Market operates a retail flower shop near the Kula Lodge on Haleakala Hwy. (377) in Kula, offering several varieties of proteas for sale. Gardens and market are open 7 a.m. to 4 p.m. daily. Free admission.

Tedeschi Vineyards. Located on Kula Hwy. (37), 9 miles south of Kula, at Ulupalakua; (808) 878-6058/(877) 878-6058/*www.maui-wine.com*. Situated on the slopes of Mt. Haleakala, this is Hawaii's only winery, originally established in 1973. Tedeschi offers four different grape wines—including two sparkling wines and a wine produced from the Carnelian grape—as well as a pineapple wine. Scenic grounds with picnicking possibilities; tasting room housed in historic, 1874 cottage. Open for wine tasting and sales daily, 9-5; winery tours at 10.30 a.m. and 1.30 p.m.

Road to Hana

Fagan Memorial. Located on Lyon's Hill, across from Hotel Hana Maui (which is situated on Hana Hwy., 360), in Hana. A paved walkway leads from the hotel, crossing over the highway, to the memorial atop the hill. It comprises a large lava-stone cross, dedicated to Paul Fagan, founder of the Hana Ranch, who died in 1959. There are also good views from the top of the hill, of the ocean and Hana Bay, and the Hana township below.

Kahanu Gardens. Located on Ulaino Rd., which goes off Hana Hwy. (360), approximately 3 miles north of Hana; (808) 248-8912/*www.ntbg.org*. Delightful, 126-acre tropical botanical gardens, now part of the National Tropical Botanical Garden. The gardens grow and display a collection of ethnobotanical plants, and are also home to one of Hawaii's largest *heiaus*, the Pi'ilanihale Heiau, some 50 feet high, dating from 1270 A.D. There is a visitor center at the gardens, offering guidebooks for self-guided walking tours of the grounds. Open 10 a.m.-2 p.m., Mon.-Fri. Admission fee: $10.00 adults, children free.

Ke'anae Arboretum. On Hana Hwy. (360). ½ mile past mile marker 16 (approximately 18 miles northwest of Hana). Features a variety of indigenous Hawaiian plants and trees, including native forest trees, tropical trees introduced to Hawaii, and cultivated Hawaiian plants. Also view irrigated taro patches, and an authentic representation of a Hawaiian rain forest. Self-guided trails. Open daily; free admission.

Hana Cultural Center. Uakea Rd. (near Keawa Place), Hana; (808) 248-8622. Small, informative museum, displaying various Hawaiian artifacts, including quilts, bowls, and historic photographs. Also visit the adjacent old courthouse and jail cells. Open 10-4, Mon.-Sat. Suggested donation: $3.00.

Hasegawa Store. 5165 Hana Hwy., Hana. Historic, family-run store, piled high with almost every imaginable item—from groceries to lawn-mowers to stereo systems. The store is in fact one of the town's leading attractions, immortalized in song and visited by a host of celebrities, including Kris Kristofferson, George Harrison, Burt Reynolds, Carol Burnett, and others. Open during business hours.

Helani Gardens. Hana Hwy. (360), Hana; (808) 248-8274. 70-acre drive-through botanical gardens, filled with lavish displays of Hawaiian plants, flowers and fruit trees. Open 10-4 daily: admission: $3.00 per person.

Oheo Gulch (Seven Sacred Pools). Off Pi'ilani Hwy. (31), approximately 10 miles south of Hana. Features more than 20 natural pools, strung along the Oheo Stream. Also offers some good hiking possibilities, with one or two trails leading past waterfalls and through bamboo forests. Views of island of Hawaii, roughly 30 miles to the south. There is, in addition, a ranger station in the gulch, with useful information for the area.

Palapala Ho'omau Church. Off Pi'ilani Hwy. (31), 12 miles southwest of Hana, in Kipahulu. Historic church, built in 1857 and situated on a bluff overlooking the ocean. There is also a small, seaside cemetery adjacent to the church, which has in it the grave of pioneer aviator Charles A. Lindbergh, and the grassy *Kipahulu Point Park*. The park has picnicking possibilities, with good views of the ocean.

Twin Falls. Off Hana Hwy. (360), 12 miles east of Paia. A dirt trail goes off the highway just past mile marker 2 (before crossing the highway bridge), journeying inland a little way, following alongside a stream, to two successive waterfalls—the Twin Falls. The two waterfalls are located approximately a mile from the trailhead (just off the highway) a quarter mile or so apart. There is also a natural pool at the foot of each of the falls, ideal for swimming.

Wailua Falls. Located along Hana Hwy. (360), 7 miles south of Hana. Picturesque, 95-foot waterfalls alongside the highway, offering good photographing opportunities.

Places to Go | Beaches

All beaches on the Hawaiian islands are public beaches, and nude bathing at public beaches is prohibited under Hawaiian state law (even though a few of them continue to be unofficial nudist beaches). Visitors to Hawaii's beaches should also be forewarned that coastal waters are subject to strong undercurrents or rip tides, especially during winter and spring, and caution is strongly advised.

West Maui

Awalua Beach. Off Hwy. 30, at mile marker 16, 5 miles south of Lahaina. Narrow roadside beach. Good swimming possibilities; sandy bottom. Also some surfing.

D.T. Fleming Beach Park. Off Hwy. 30, at mile marker 31, approximately a mile east of Kapalua. Long, sandy beach, bordered by ironwood trees and shallow sand dunes. Offers picnic tables, barbecue grills, showers, restrooms, and public phone. Some surfing possibilities; unsafe for swimming due to dangerous undercurrents.

Hanakao'o Beach Park. Situated half-mile north of Wahikuli State Wayside Park (approximately 2½ miles north of Lahaina), off Hwy. 30. Offers picnic tables, showers and restroom facilities. Safe swimming conditions. The beach borders Ka'anapali Beach to the north, and is a good place to park and stroll along the beach at Ka'anapali.

Honokowai Beach Park. Located a mile north of Ka'anapali Beach Resort, off Lower Honoapi'ilani Rd., in Honokowai. Rocky beach with a large, grassy area with picnic tables. Also showers and restrooms, and parking facilities. Some snorkeling and swimming.

Honolua Bay. Off Honoapi'ilani Hwy. (30), ½ past mile marker 33, adjoining to the east of Mokuleia Bay (see above), and reached by way of a dirt road from the highway, passing through pineapple fields. This is one of the most popular surfing spots on the island, featured on covers of surfing magazines. Good place to watch world-class surfers, especially during winter months.

Ka'anapali Beach. 4 miles north of Lahaina, at the Ka'anapali Beach Resort, off Honoapi'ilani Hwy. (30). This is one of Hawaii's most popular beaches, 3 miles long, fronting on the Ka'anapali resorts, extending from the Hyatt Regency north to the Sheraton and beyond. Offers safe swimming in summer, and some of the best snorkeling on the island, near Black Rock, at the north end of the beach. The beach can be accessed by way of any of several different public access roads; however, parking is limited.

Kahana Beach. 2 miles north of Honokowai Beach (3 miles

north of Ka'anapali), off Lower Honoapi'ilani Rd. in Kahana. Features a protective reef just offshore, with safe swimming conditions. Also offers views of Molokai and Lanai. No beach facilities.

Kapalua Beach. Situated at Kapalua, bordering Kapalua Bay Hotel, with a public access just past Napili Kai Beach Club, off Lower Honoapi'ilani Rd. Beautiful, white-sand cove with superb views of the island of Molokai. Offers good diving and snorkeling possibilities and safe swimming. Beach facilities include restrooms and showers; limited parking.

Launiupoko State Wayside Beach Park. Located 2½ miles south of Lahaina, off Hwy. 30, near mile marker 18. Rocky beach with a wading pool for children. Offers views of Kaho'olawe, Lanai and Molokai. Beach facilities include picnic tables, barbecue grills, showers, restrooms, and parking area.

Mokuleia Beach (Slaughterhouse Beach). Situated at the head of Mokuleia Bay, approximately a mile northeast of D.T. Fleming Beach, just past mile marker 32 on Hwy. 30, with a handful of trails leading from the highway down to the beach. The beach is part of the *Honolua-Mokuleia Bay Marine Life Conservation District*, quite popular, in summer, with snorkeling and board surfing enthusiasts. During winter, the strong undercurrents make the ocean here unsafe for water activities. No facilities.

Napili Bay. Situated 5 miles north of Ka'anapali, and reached by way of Lower Honoapi'ilani Rd., then either Hui Drive or Napili Place, with public access roads leading down from these to the beach. The beach is a lovely, white-sand, crescent-shaped beach, bordered by condominium resorts. Offers excellent swimming and snorkeling in calm weather.

Papalaua State Wayside Beach. Located 4½ miles west of Ma'alaea (approximately 10 miles southeast of Lahaina), off Honoapi'ilani Hwy. (30), between mile markers 11 and 12. Roadside beach, bordered by *kiawe* trees. Offers views of the island of Kaho'olawe. Also picnicking, swimming, snorkeling, and surfing.

Puamana Beach Park. Located just south of Lahaina, off Hwy. 30. Narrow, sandy beach with picnic tables and parking facilities. Offers good swimming in summer, and promising surfing conditions just north of the beach.

Punahoa Beach. Off Honoapi'ilani Hwy. (30), at mile marker 14, approximately 7 miles southeast of Lahaina. Popular white-sand beach, with excellent snorkeling possibilities. Also safe swimming conditions in summer. The beach is bordered by *kiawe* trees.

Ukumehame Beach Park. Half mile west of Papalaua Beach (see above), off Honoapi'ilani Hwy. (30), at mile marker 12. Rocky beach with large grassy area, ideal for picnicking. Some fishing possibilities.

Wahikuli State Wayside Park. 2 miles north of Lahaina, along Hwy. 30. Popular roadside beach park with small, sandy area and rocky shoreline. Facilities include picnic tables, showers and restrooms. Some swimming and snorkeling possibilities.

Southwest Coast

Ahihi-Kinau Natural Area Reserve. Located a mile south of Oneloa Beach (approximately 4 miles south of Makena), off Makena Rd. Offers excellent scuba diving and snorkeling possibilities. Fishing, hunting and removal of coral and lava prohibited. Unsafe ocean conditions during high surf. No facilities.

Kalama Beach Park. Off S. Kihei Rd., Kihei, ½ mile south of mile marker 3. Shoreline park with picnic tables, restrooms, basketball and tennis courts, soccer field, and baseball diamond. Also parking facilities.

Kalepolepo Beach Park. Located just south of mile marker 1 on S. Kihei Rd., Kihei. Small, sandy beach with safe swimming for children. Showers and restroom facilities, and parking area.

Kamaole Beach Parks (I, II and III). Located off S. Kihei Rd., just past mile marker 4, south of Kihei. Three consecutive beaches, separated only by rocky outcroppings. All three beaches offer safe swimming and good sunbathing possibilities. Kamaole I also offers bodysurfing possibilities, and Kamaole III features a children's playground. Showers and restroom facilities at all three beaches.

Keawakapu Beach. Situated less than a mile south of Kamaole Beach III (approximately 5 miles south of Kihei), and reached by way of one of two access roads—from the intersection of S. Kihei Rd. and Kilohana Dr., or from the end of S. Kihei Rd., ¼ mile past mile marker 6. The beach has a sandy bottom and offers good swimming, body boarding and snorkeling possibilities. No facilities.

La Perouse Bay. Situated 1½ miles south of Ahihi-Kinau Natural Area Reserve, at the end of Makena Rd. Undeveloped beach area. Offers good scuba diving and snorkeling possibilities, but is generally unsafe for swimming. Ruins of ancient fishing village nearby, on the inland side of the historic Hoapili Trail which heads out eastward.

Ma'alaea Beach. Situated just north of Kihei, off N. Kihei Rd. (Hwy. 31). Three-mile-long beach, swept by strong afternoon winds. Offers beachcombing and jogging possibilities; also some surfing in summer. Swimming and windsurfing are not advisable due to the adverse ocean and wind conditions. No facilities.

Maipoina Oe Iau. Located off S. Kihei Rd. in Kihei, a half-mile south of the intersection of Hwy. 350. Popular windsurfing spot; also offers safe swimming conditions in the summer months. Whale watching in winter and spring. Facilities include restrooms and picnic tables.

Makena Landing Beach Park. Just to the south of Po'olenalena

Beach (see above). Off Makena Rd., approximately ½ mile from the end of Makena Alanui, at Makena. Small, rocky beach, which is also a popular starting point for scuba diving expeditions. Beach facilities include showers, restrooms and a parking area.

Maluaka Beach Park. At the Maui Prince Hotel, ½ mile south of Makena Landing, accessed from Makena Rd. (which is a continuation of Makena Alanui), in Makena. The beach is wide, crescent-shaped, and backed by shallow, grassy sand dunes and groves of *kiawe* trees. Offers safe swimming conditions, and showers and restroom facilities. Also parking area.

Mokapu Beach. Located at Renaissance Beach Resort at Wailea; reached by way of a public access road, just to the south of the Renaissance, off Wailea Alanui. Small cove, with a sandy bottom, ideal for swimming and bodysurfing. Also promising snorkeling on calm days. No public facilities.

Oneloa Beach (Makena Beach). Situated off Makena Rd., 3 miles south of the intersection of Kaukahi Rd. and Makena Alanui; reached by way of a dirt road that goes off Makena Rd., approximately ¼ mile, toward the ocean. Long, white-sand beach in idyllic setting; one of the southwest coast's loveliest beaches. Offers good bodysurfing possibilities; also snorkeling along the north end of the beach, just around Red Hill. Swimming is not encouraged due to unpredictable ocean currents. No facilities. The beach is also known as Big Beach.

Oneuli Beach (Black Sand Beach). Located on the north side of Pu'u Ola'i (Red Hill); accessed by way of a dirt road that goes off Makena Rd. (continuation of Makena Alanui), approximately 3 miles south of the intersection of Kaukahi Rd. and Makena Alanui. The beach is fronted by a coral reef, making it unsafe for swimming. No beach facilities.

Palauea Beach. Located ¼ mile south of Polo Beach, off Wailea Alanui; reached by way of a public access road along the shoreline from Polo Beach. Lovely, secluded, sandy beach, bordered by *kiawe* trees. Offers some swimming and bodysurfing possibilities. No beach facilities.

Polo Beach. Off Kaukahi Rd. (which goes off Wailea Alanui, just past Kea Lani Hotel) in Wailea. Offers good swimming, snorkeling and bodysurfing; also superb views of Kaho'olawe and Molokini. Showers, restrooms, and parking facilities.

Po'olenalena Beach Park (Paipu Beach). Situated 2 miles south of Wailea, off Makena Alanui. Undeveloped sandy beach, backed by low sand dunes and *kiawe* trees. Good swimming possibilities, except during high surf or kona storms. No facilities.

Pu'uolai Beach (Little Beach). Off Makena Rd., roughly 3 miles south of the intersection of Kaukahi Rd.; accessed from the north end of Oneloa Beach (see above), over a rocky outcropping. The beach itself is small, sandy, and one of the most popular nudist beaches on Maui. It offers safe swimming conditions, as well as some good bodysurfing possibilities.

Ulua Beach. Located just south of the Renaissance Beach Resort at Wailea, off Wailea Alanui. Offers good swimming and bodysurfing possibilities, as well as snorkeling in calm seas. Showers, restrooms, parking area.

Wailea Beach. At the Grand Hyatt and Four Seasons resort hotels in Wailea, with public access off Wailea Alanui, passing between the two resorts and down to the beach. Wailea Beach is a beautiful, white-sand beach, with good swimming, snorkeling and bodysurfing possibilities. Beach facilities include showers and restrooms; also parking area.

Central Maui

H.P. Baldwin Park. Located just west of Paia, off Hana Hwy. (36), at mile marker 6. Well-liked beach, especially popular with swimmers, body-surfers and picnickers. Offers picnic tables, showers, restrooms, a pavilion, and baseball and soccer fields.

Ho'okipa Beach Park. Off Hana Hwy. (36), 2 miles east of Paia. This is one of the most popular windsurfing and surfing spots on the island, and the site of several national and international windsurfing competitions. Not suitable for swimming.

Kanaha Beach Park. Situated off Alahao St., near the Kahului Airport, in Kahului. Popular sandy beach, bordered by *kiawe* trees. Offers safe swimming for children, and good windsurfing and surfing possibilities. Picnic tables, barbecue grills, showers and restrooms.

Waihe'e Beach Park. Situated near the Waiehu Municipal Golf Course, off Halewaiu Rd. (which goes off Kahekili Hwy., 340), in Waihe'e. Narrow, gray-sand beach, frequented primarily by fishermen. Some beachcombing possibilities. Also picnic tables, showers, restrooms, and parking facilities.

Waiehu Beach Park. Located at the end of Lower Waiehu Beach Rd., which goes off Kahekili Hwy. (340), in Waiehu. Narrow, sandy beach, frequented primarily by fishermen. Beachcombing. No facilities.

Hana

Hamoa Beach Park. Located at the head of Mokae Cove, off Haneo'o Rd. (which goes off Hwy. 31), 2½ miles south of Hana. The beach is used almost exclusively by guests of the Hotel Hana Maui. Offers good surfing and bodysurfing possibilities; also safe swimming in calm weather. No public access.

Hana Beach Park. Situated along the southeast end of Hana Bay, and reached on Keawa Place, which goes off Hana Hwy. (360). Popular local beach; offers one of the safest swimming areas in East Maui. Also good snorkeling possibilities in the section between the beach pier and lighthouse. Picnic tables, showers, restrooms.

Kaihalulu Beach (Red Sand Beach). Off Wakea Rd., Hana; reached by way of a trail leading from the south end of Wakea Rd. down to the beach. Small beach area, comprising largely a volcanic cinder. Unsafe for swimming.

Koki Beach Park. Situated approximately 1½ miles southeast of Hana, off Haneo'o Rd., which goes off Pi'ilani Hwy. (31). Popular surfing and bodysurfing beach, bordered by ironwood trees. Picnic tables, barbecue pits. Unsafe for swimming.

Pa'iloa Beach. At the Waianapanapa State Park (2 miles north of Hana), off Hana Hwy., at mile marker 32. Small, black-sand beach with picnic area. Swimming not advised due to prevailing, strong ocean currents.

Tours and Activities

Helicopter Tours

Helicopter tours are quite popular on Maui, and a good way to see the island, with several different companies offering flights over West Maui, the Haleakala crater, the Hana area and other parts of the island. Tours originate at the Kahului Heliport in Kahului, and tour companies, typically, utilize any of three different types of helicopters—the Aero-Star, a 6-seater, with all seats by the windows, offering all passengers good views; the Hughes 500, a 4-seater that also offers window seating to all passengers; and the Bell Jet Ranger, another 4-seater that has only three window seats, with one passenger being confined to a center seat and, consequently, lesser views. Tours last anywhere from 20 minutes to an hour, and cost $79-$250 per person. For reservations and more information, contact any of the following:

Alexair Helicopters. 108 Kahului Heliport, Kahului; (808) 871-0792/(800)462-2281/(888) 418-8455/*www.helitour.com*; offers scenic helicopter tours, in its Birds of Paradise helicopters, of Maui's most spectacular sights, including the tropical rainforests of the east coast of the island and the Haleakala Crater. Prices range from $79.00 for a 20-minute flight tour to $250.00 for an hour-long tour. Online booking discounts available.

Blue Hawaiian Helicopters. 105 Kahului Heliport, Kahului, (808) 871-8844/(800) 745-2583/*www.bluehawaiian.com*; aerial tours in the roomy, state-of-the-art EC130-84 ECO-Stars as well as the A-Star touring helicopters. Operates from Maui, Kauai and the Big Island, offering tours of all three islands as well as Molokai. On Maui, tours range from 30 minutes to 1½ hours, taking in the West Maui mountains or Haleakala, Hana, Molokai, or even the entire island of Maui. Also custom-designed tours. Prices range from $125.00 for 30 a 30 minute tour to $280.00 for 1½ hours of sightseeing.

Air Maui. 500 Ala Moana Blvd., Ste. 400, Honolulu (departs from Kahului Heliport on Maui); (808) 441-4500/*www.mauihelicopters.org*. Offers fully-narrated aerial tours of Maui's sights, including Haleakala, Hana, Molokini, and West Maui, in its air-conditioned American Eurocopter ASTAR helicopters. Prices range from $130.00 for a 30-minute flight over the West Maui mountains to $253.00 for a 1-hour flight taking in the entire island. Reservations are also made through Hawaii Travel Network; (808) 356-1800/(888) 349-7888/*www.hawaiitravelnetwork.com*.

Mauiscape Helicopters. 415 Dairy Rd., #B, Kahului; (808) 877-7272/(888) 440-7272/*www.mauiscape.net*. Scenic aerial tours of Maui's popular sights on board 6-seater Eurocopter A-Star and 4-seater Eurocopter EC120 helicopters. 45-minute to 1-hour tours, taking in the Hana rainforest and Haleakala crater, as well as complete island. Cost: $180.00-$200.00 for a 45-minute flight to $235.00-$250.00 for 1-hour flight, depending on the type of helicopter used.

Sunshine Helicopter Tours. 1 Kahului Airport Rd., Kahului, (808) 871-0722/(800) 469-3000/(800) 622-3144/*www.sunshinehelicopters.com*; air tours in air-conditioned luxury aboard Black Beauty helicopters, outfitted with SkyCam video systems. Tours range from those of Maui's premier attractions, such as Upcountry and Haleakala and the spectacular Hana coast, to Molokai's sheer sea cliffs at Kalaupapa. Prices range from $115.00 for a West Maui tour to $370.00 for deluxe Molokai tour in first class seating. Discounts for online bookings.

Sightseeing Tours

Akina Aloha Tours. 140 Alahele Pl., P.O. Box 933, Kihei, HI 96753; (808) 879-2828/(800) 800-3989/*www.akinatours.com*. Offers a variety of guided tours, including Upcountry and the Haleakala crater, the Road to Hana, Iao Valley, the Maui Ocean Center and historical Maui. Tours are conducted in vans, minibuses, motor coaches, or even limousines, and include stops for lunch. Cost of tours ranges from $70.00 adults ($50.00 children) for the Sunrise at Haleakala Tour to $95.00 adults ($70.00 children) for the Explore Hana Tour.

Polynesian Adventure Tours. 273 Dairy Rd.., Kahului; (808) 877-

4242/(800) 622-3011/*www.polyad.com*. Offers customized motor coach and mini coach day tours of Haleakala and the Iao Valley and Hana; also Haleakala sunrise tours . Cost of tours ranges from $65.00 per person for the Haleakala tour to $85.00 for the Hana tour.

Robert's Hawaii. 711 Kaonawai Pl., Kahului; (808) 871-6226/(800) 831-5541/*www.robertshawaii.com*. Narrated scenic tours of Haleakala and the Iao Valley and Lahaina, as well as adventure tours of Hana. Air-conditioned motor coaches. Cost of tours: $45.00-$89.00 per person.

Sugarcane Train (Lahaina-Ka'anapali Railroad). 975 Limahana Pl., Suite 203, Lahaina. Departs and arrives at rail depots at cnr. Lahainaluna Rd. and Hinau Rd. in Lahaina, and cnr. Honoapi'ilani Hwy. (30) and Pu'ukolii Rd., Pu'ukolii (near Ka'anapali; (808) 661-0080(808) 667-6851/(800) 499-2307/*www.sugarcanetrain.com*. Historic, 19th-century steam train with open-air coaches. Operates between Lahaina and Ka'anapali, along a 6-mile stretch of track, daily from 10.15 a.m. until 4 p.m., passing by sugarcane fields and scenic vistas. Trains depart from each end—from the Lahaina and Ka'anapali stations—approximately every 1¼ to 2 hours; train rides are around 1 hour each way, with live, entertaining commentary enroute. Also "Dinner Train" on Thursdays, offering all-you-can-eat Hawaiian-style barbecue and live Hawaiian music and dancing, departing Ka'anapali at 5 p.m. Round trip fare: $18.95 adults, $12.95 children (3-12 yrs., under 3 yrs, free). Dinner Train: $76.00 adults, $43.00 children.

Temptation Tours. 21 Ahinahina Pl., P.O. Box 454, Kula, HI 96790; (808) 877-8888/(800) 817-1234/*www.temptationtours.com*. Custom sightseeing tours of Hana and Haleakala in luxury limovans, for groups of 6-8 persons, combining helicopter rides and including lunch. Tours originate in Kahului and are narrated. Cost of tours ranges from $149.00 per person for the Hana Picnic Tour to $259.00 per person for the Hana Sky-Trek or the Summit Safari.

Hiking Tours

Hawaiian Bicycle Experience. P.O. Box 1874, Kihei, HI 96753; (808) 874-1929. Guided hiking trips to pristine waterfalls and black-sand beaches; also hiking in Maui's Upcountry. 6-hour hikes. Cost: $50.00 per person.

Hike Maui. 285 Hukilike St., Ste. B-104, Kahului; (808) 879-5270/(866) 324-MAUI/*www.hikemaui.com*. Several guided day hikes, from easy to strenuous, leading through rainforests to waterfalls; also trails through volcanic craters and along mountain ridges and rugged coastlines. Also offered is a hike with some snorkeling and kayaking. Hikes includes motor transport to and from trail-heads. Cost ranges from $65.00 for the Short Waterfall Adventure to $270.00 for the Heli Hike and Waterfalls (which includes a helicopter ride).

Maui Eco-Adventures. 180 Dickenson, #102, Lahaina; (808) 661-7720/(877) 661-7720/*www.ecomaui.com*. Guided hikes through the barren moonscape of the Haleakala crater, as well as through rainforests near Hana, on the eastern part of Maui, leading to waterfalls. Transportation to the trailheads is provided on air-conditioned vans. Also some hike-kayak tours, and bike tours. Cost of hike tours on the island ranges from $125.00 to around $145.00.

Maui Hiking Safaris. P.O. Box 11198, Lahaina, HI 96761; (808) 573-0168(888) 445-3963/*www.mauihikingsafaris.com*. Half- and full-day hikes, ranging from easy to strenuous, and accompanied by informative narrative on history and flora. Trails wind through rainforests and valleys to waterfalls, and along mountain ridges. Transportation to the hiking locales, day packs, water and meals are provided. Cost: $59.00-$109.00.

Bicycling Tours

Bike It Maui. (866) 776-2453/*www.bikeitmaui.com*. 38-mile, guided sunrise bike tours from the Haleakala summit down to the coastal town of Paia. Includes helmets, gloves, weather jackets and pants. Also full breakfast. Cost: $109.00 per person.

Maui Downhill Bicycle Safaris. 199 Dairy Rd., Kahului; (808) 871-2155/(800) 535-2453/*www.mauidownhill.com*. This is the original Maui downhill bike tours company, offering morning and afternoon guided tours down the slopes of Haleakala on custom-built chrome bikes, with safety helmets, windbreakers and insulated gloves provided on all tours. Selection of tours, ranging from 22 miles to 38 miles downhill. Tour prices: $75.00-$108.00.

Maui Mountain Cruiser's. 15 S. Wakea Ave., Kahului; (808) 871-6014/(800) 232-6284/*www.mauimountaincruisers.com*. Sunrise and midday rides, down the slopes of Haleakala; includes rain gear, gloves, and round-trip transportation. Also, continental breakfast, and lunch on the way down the mountain. Tour cost: sunrise ride, $130.00; midday ride, $125.00.

Maui Mountain Riders. 220 Lalo Bay #5, Kahului; (808) 242-9739(800) 706-7700/*www.mountainriders.com*. Guided and self-guided downhill bike tours, from the Haleakala summit, 38 miles down to the ocean. Volcano chrome cruisers and windbreaker jackets and pants as well as gloves are provided. Also round-trip transportation in air-conditioned vans and continental breakfast are included. Cost: $59.95-$115.00.

MAUI | Tours and Activities

Maui Sunriders Bike Company. 71 Baldwin Ave. #B-3, P.O. Box 790921, Paia, HI 96779; (808) 579-8970/(866) 500-2453/*www. mauibikeride.com*. Self-guided Haleakala downhill bike tours, from the summit down to Paia on Maui's north coast. Bike locks, backpacks, rain gear and gloves are provided; also van ride to the summit. Tour cost: $44.95-$69.95; cost of renting bike and equipment only: $29.95.

Haleakala Bike Company. 810 Haiku Rd., Ste. 120, Hailu; (808) 575-9575/(888) 922-2453/*www.bikemaui.com*. Self-guided downhill bike tours, from the Haleakala summit, down the Haleakala Highway, descending 3,000 feet in 10 miles, curving around 29 switchbacks. The bike tour takes in Upcountry locales such as Makawao, Tedeschi Vineyards, and Keokea. Some tours include a van tour of the Haleakala park. Good selection of rental bikes. Tour prices range from $65.00-$75.00.

Horseback Rides and Tours

Haleakala on Horseback. (808) 871-0990/*www.haleakala-onhorseback.com*. 4- and 6-hour horseback rides through the Haleakala Crater; includes continental breakfast and lunch at the Kapalaoa Cabin on the other side of the crater. Cost: $155-$195 per person.

Hana Ranch. Hana; (808) 248-8211/*www.hotelhanamaui. com*. 1- and 2-hour horseback rides along the Hana coast and on ranchland; some of the rides include barbecues. Cost: $50-$90 per person.

Ironwood Ranch. Napili; (808) 669-4991/*www.ironwoodranch. com*. Offers a variety of trail rides to suit all levels of riders; rides are conducted primarily in the West Maui area, on mountain, rainforest and ranchland, and range from ½ hour to 2 hours. Cost: $80-$110 per person.

Makena Stables. 7299 Makena Rd., Makena; (808) 879-0244/ *makenastables.com*. Offers 2½-hour and 3-hour morning as well as sunset rides on the slopes of Ulupalakua Ranch in Upcountry, with views of La Perouse Bay. Cost: 2½-hour morning ride, $135.00; 3-hour sunset ride, $160.00.

Pony Express. Haleakala Crater Rd., Kula; (808) 667-2200/*www. ponyexpresstours.com*. Guided, 4- and 6-hour rides through the Haleakala Crater; includes lunch. Also 1- to 2½-hour ranch rides in Maui's Upcountry. Tour cost: Haleakala Crater rides, $170-$210; ranch rides, $70-$120.

Thompson Ranch. RR 2, P.O. Box 203, Kula, HI 96790; (808) 878-1910/*www.thompsonranchmaui.com*. Offers 1½-hour trail rides on a cattle ranch in Upcountry. Cost: $75.00 per person.

Boat Tours and Snorkeling Excursions

Atlantis Submarines. Lahaina Harbor, Slip 18, Lahaina: (808) 667-2224/(808) 667-6604/(800) 548-6262/*www.atlantisadventures. com*. Unique underwater excursions aboard a 65 foot submarine, exploring more than 100 feet below the ocean surface. Large view-port for viewing hundreds of fish, sea turtles and other exotic sea creatures amidst a coral reef just offshore from Lahaina. One-hour excursions, offered daily from 9 a.m. until 2 p.m., on the hour. Tour cost: $80.00 adults, $42.00 children.

Blue Water Rafting. 1280 S. Kihei Rd., Ste. 205, Kihei; (808) 879-7238/*www.bluewaterrafting.com*. Variety of snorkeling excur-sions on board 6-passenger and 24-passenger rafts. Includes trips to Molokini and Maui's south shore, as well as whale-watching excursions. Cost ranges from $45.00 for the Molokini Express snor-keling trip to $115.00 for the 5½-hour Kanaio Coast and Molokini sightseeing and snorkeling tour.

Captain Nemo's. 2349 S. Kihei Rd., Kihei; (808) 661-5555/*www. scubashack.com*. Daily snorkeling and scuba diving excursions to Molokini and around Kihei coast, with two-tank dives. Cost: $69.00 per person.

Friendly Charters. 187 Haulani St., Pukalani (departs from Ma'alaea Harbor, Slip 76, Ma'alaea); (808) 244-1979/(888) 983-8080/*www.mauisnorkeling.com*. Snorkeling excursions to Molokini and Turtle Reef on board a 53-foot, double-decker catamaran; also whale watching during season. Snorkeling trips include snorkel-ing equipment. Continental breakfast and a deli-style buffet lunch are also provided. Price for snorkeling tour: $88.00 adults, $58.00 children. Discount for booking online.

Island Marine Activities. 658 Front St., Ste. 101, Lahaina: (808) 661-8397/(800) 275-6969/(877) 500-6284/*www.mauiprincess. com*. Ocean cruises, including *Maui Princess* dinner cruise; also whale-watching tours, snorkeling and scuba diving excursions to Molokini, and Molokai ferry. Prices range from $19.00 ($12.50 chil-dren) for an early morning whale watching trip to $79.00 ($59.00 children) for a *Maui Princess* dinner cruise.

Maui Classic Charters. P.O. Box 959, Kihei, HI 96753 (boats de-part from Ma'alaea Harbor, Ma'alaea); (808) 879-8188/(800) 736-5740/*www,mauicharters.com*. Morning and afternoon snorkeling excursions to Molokini, on board a 55-foot, glass-bottom catama-ran; continental breakfast and barbecue lunch on the morning trip, and lunch with beer and wine on the afternoon tour. Also whale-watching excursions, including some snorkeling. Snorkeling gear is included on tours. Cost: morning adventure, $84.00; afternoon snorkeling trips, $42.00; whale-watching tour, $42.00.

Ocean Riders. P.O. Box 967, Lahaina, HI 96767; (808) 661-3586/(877) 321-4429/*www.mauioceanriders.com*. Full-day snorkeling trips to Lanai, circling the island, with 3 snorkeling stops; includes continental breakfast and buffet lunch. Also private charters available. Tour cost: $130.00 adults, $80.00 children.

Pacific Whale Foundation. Ma'alaea Harbor Village, 300 Ma'alaea R., Ste. 211, Ma'alaea; (808) 249-8811/(800) 942-5311/ *www.pacificwhale.org*. Marine conservation organization, offering whale-watching and marine eco-tours on board catamarans; sunset cocktail cruises, dinner cruises, and snorkeling tours to Molokini and Lanai. Cost: snorkeling tours, $79.00 (children, $29.95); whale watches, $29.95 adults (children, $15.00); sunset cruise, $49.95 adults (children, $39.95); dinner cruise, $79.95 adults (children, $49.95).

Paragon Sailing Charters. 5229 Lower Kula Rd., Kula; (808) 244-2087/(800) 441-2087/*www.sailmaui.com*. Offers sailing and snorkeling tours of Molokini, Lanai and the Coral Gardens near Ma'alaea Bay; also champagne sunset sailing excursions near Lahaina, and whale watches in season. Cost: sunset sail or Coral Gardens snorkeling, $43.00 adults, $28.00 children; Molokini tour, $72.00 adults, $36.00 children; Lanai tour, $127.00 adults, $84.00 children.

Island Star Sailing Excursions. P.O. Box 381, Lahaina, HI 96767; (808) 669-7827/(888) 677-7238/*www.islandstarsailing.com*. Offers private sailing charters in the islands, from 2-hour sunset sails to week-long sailing excursions around the islands aboard a 10-passenger cutter. Cost: $500.00 per hour.

Prince Kuhio. 831 Eha St., Ste. 101. Wailuku (departs from Ma'alaea Harbor in Ma'alaea); (808) 242-8777/(800) 468-1287/ *www.mvprince.com*. Half-day snorkeling trip to Molokini, including continental breakfast and a luncheon buffet with beer, wine and beverages; also whale watches. Tour cost: snorkeling trip, $81.00 adults and $49.00 children; whale-watching trip, $32.00 adults, $21.00 children.

Seafire Charters. P.O. Box 1864, Kihei, HI 96753 (departs from the Kihei Boat Ramp); (808) 879-2201/*www.molokinisnorkeling. com*. Daily snorkeling excursions to Molokini, departing at 7.30 a.m. and 10.30 a.m.; includes all snorkeling equipment, and continental breakfast and drinks. Also boat tours of Turtle Town. Cost: $49.00 per person.

Scotch Mist. P.O. Box 831, Lahaina, HI 96767 (departs from the Lahaina Harbor, Slip 2); (808) 661-0386/*www.scotchmistsailingcharters.com*. Offers snorkeling and sailing excursions along the West Maui coast, as well as sunset sails with complimentary beer, wine, fruit juice and champagne. Also whale watches in season, and private charters. Cost: $65.00 for snorkeling excursions; $37.50 for sailing tours; $45.00 for sunset/cocktail sails.

Trilogy Excursions. 180 Lahainaluna Rd., Lahaina; (808) 661-4743/(888) 628-1800/*www.sailtrilogy.com*. Snorkeling expeditions to Ka'anapali and Molokini, and all-day touring, snorkeling and kayaking trips to Lanai. Cost ranges from $49.00 for a whale-watching excursion to $250 for a tour of Lanai with kayaking; children are half-price on all tours.

Scuba Diving

Scuba diving is a popular recreational sport on Maui—especially around Molokini, just offshore from Maui—and at the nearby island of Lanai, with several different companies offering introductory scuba dives as well as tank dives for certified divers. Dives are offered both from the shore and from boats. Rates range from $65-$135 for introductory dives, and $80-$180 for tank dives; equipment is generally included.

Ed Robinson's Diving Adventures. P.O. Box 616. Kihei, HI 96753; (808) 879-3584/(800 635-1273/www.mauiscuba.com. Offers diving adventures for certified divers, to Molokini and Maui's south coast, as well as Lanai. Also snorkeling tours along the south Maui coast. Cost: $90.00 for snorkeling trips, $120.00-$175.00 for diving excursions.

Extended Horizons. 94 Kupuohi #A-1, Lahaina; (808) 667-0611(888) 348-3628/*www.scubadivemaui.com*. Boat-based dive tours around Maui and Lanai. Cost: $89.00-$129.00.

Isana Ocean Sports. 207 Puapihi St., Lahaina; (808) 661-9950/*www.isana.com*. Scuba diving and snorkeling tours. Also diving certification and surfing lessons, and equipment rentals. Dives from $80.00 to $150.00, open water dive certification $500.00.

Lahaina Divers. 143 Dickenson St., Lahaina; (808) 667-7496/(800) 998-3483/*www.lahainadivers.com*. Diving excursions to the Molokini Crater, the Cathedrals of Lanai, and Turtle Reef. Also open water diver certification. Training courses with dive excursions range from $39.00 to $399.00; dives at Molokini Crater and Turtle Reef range from $79.00 to 179.00.

Maui Dive Shop. 1455 S. Kihei Rd., Kihei; (808) 875-0333/(800) 542-3483/*www.mauidiveshop.com*. Snorkeling and diving center, offering daily charters to snorkeling and dive sites at Molokini and Lanai. Also equipment rental. Cost: $34.95-$59.00 for snorkeling, and $99.95-$120.95 for dives.

Maui Scuba Diving with Turtle Reef Divers. P.O. Box 13085, Lahaina, HI 96761; (877) 873-4837/*www.mauiscubadiving.com*. Boat-beach scuba trips from Lahaina, Ma'alaea Harbor and Kihei to Turtle Reef, the Molokini Crater and the Cathedrals of Lanai. Also equipment rentals. Maui dive packages range from $120.00 to $260.00.

Mike Severn's Diving. P.O. Box 627, Kihei, HI 96753; (808) 879-

6596/*www.mikesevernsdiving.com*. Boat-based dive excursions to select diving sites around Maui. Cost: $135.00.

Scuba Mike. (808) 250-5494/*www.scubamike.net*. Dive tours and training courses; also scooter dives and kayak tours. Prices range from $65.00 for a regular dive and $99.00 for a scooter dive, to $320.00 for open water certification.

Sportfishing

There are more than a half-dozen companies offering sportfishing charters around Maui, operating primarily from Lahaina and Ma'alaea. Charters, typically, last 4-8 hours, with prices ranging from $100-$180 per person for shared or group charters, to $550-$950 for exclusive trips; rates include all equipment, as well as beverages on the trips. For more information, and reservations, contact any of the following:

Aerial Sportfishing Charters. Lahaina, (808) 667-9089/*www. aerialsportfishingcharters.com*. Deep sea fishing for marlin, ahi, mahi mahi and ono. 4-, 6-- and 8-hour trips, both private and share boat. Cost: $120-$175 share boat; $650-$850 private charter.

Carol Ann Charters. Ma'alaea, (808) 877-2181. Offers private fishing charters, 4 to 8 hours. Cost ranges from $500-$700.

Finest Kind Sportfishing., Lahaina. (808) 661-0338/*www. fishingmaui.com*. Three-quarters- and full-day sportfishing charters, targeting marlin, ahi, and other deep sea fish. Five fully-equipped boats available. Cost: $160-$175 share boat; $850-$900 private.

Hinatea Sportfishing. Lahaina, (808) 667-7548/*www.fishmaui. com*. 4- to 8-hour trips. Rates: $140-$180 in a share boat; $750-$950 for a private charter.

Lahaina Charter Boats. Lahaina, (808) 667-6672. Offers 4-, 6- and 8-hour fishing charters, private and share boat; 6 people maximum. Rates: $100-$150 on a share boat; $560-$800 for private charters.

Luckey Strike Charters. Lahaina, (808) 661-4606/*www.luckey-strike.com*. 4-, 6- and 8-hour charters on board a 50-foot sportfishing vessel. Marlin, ahi, mahi mahi and Hawaiian salmon. Cost: share boat, $125-$179; private charter, $675-$895.

Rascal Sportfishing Charters. Ma'alaea, (808) 874-8633/*www. rascalcharters.com*. 6- and 8-hour fishing charters, private and share boat, with a 6-person maximum. Trolling and deep sea fishing. Targeted catch: marlin, ahi, spear fish, ono and mahi mahi. Cost: $175-$190 on a share boat; $850-$950 for a private charter.

Action Sportfishing on Start Me Up. Lahaina Harbor, Slip 36, Lahaina; (808) 667-2774/*www.sportfishingmaui.com*. Fishing charters on board a modern, tournament-equipped, 42-foot, air-conditioned sportfishing yacht. Targeted catch: marlin, mahi mahi, ahi, ono, spear fish. Charters range from 2 hours to full day. Cost: $99-$179 on a share boat; $299-$899 for a private charter.

Fish Maui. (808) 879-3789/*www.fishmaui.com*. Sportfishing referrals for charter boats. Also information and advice on shore and reef fishing on Maui.

Sportfish Hawaii. 575 Cooke St., #A3315, Honolulu, HI 96813; (877) 388-1376/*www.sportfishhawaii.com*. Sportfishing guide and store, arranging charters and making referrals for sportfishing trips in the islands, including Maui. Also offers charts and maps of fishing grounds, and information on sportfishing related events and tournaments.

Strike Zone Fishing. Ma'alaea Harbor, Slip 64, Ma'alaea; (808) 879-4485. Daily sportfishing trips for deep sea fishing and trolling for marlin and mahi mahi, as well as bottom fishing for snapper. 6-hour trips, 6.30 a.m.-12.30 p.m. Cost: $150.00 per person.

Windsurfing

Windsurfing is one of Maui's foremost recreational water sports, especially popular at Ho'okipa, near Paia, at Kanaha Beach Park at Kahului, and off the coast of Kihei. Introductory lessons as well as sailboard rentals are available from several different local companies, with rates ranging from $45-$50 per day for equipment rental to $260-$290 for a week, and $55-$80 for lessons. Some companies also offer complete windsurf packages, with accommodations handy to a surf beach, rental car, and windsurfing equipment; cost usually ranges from $120-$455 daily to $539-$749 weekly. For availability of equipment, lessons, and more information, contact any of the following:

Hawaiian Island Surf and Sport. 415 Dairy Rd., Kahului; (800) 231-6958/*www.hawaiianisland.com*. Sailboard, kite board and surfboard rentals sales; also lessons. Full-service shop.

Hawaiian Sailboard Techniques. P.O. Box 791199, Paia, HI 96779; (808) 871-5423/(800) 968-5423/*www.hstwindsurfing.com*. Lessons at windsurfing school owned and operated by World Cup pro Alan Cadiz. $79-$279.

Hi-Tech Surf Sports. 425 Koloa St., Kahului; (808) 877-2111/ *www.htmaui.com*. Board and sail rentals and sales. Also lessons.

Kanahakai Maui. 96 Amala, Kahului; (808) 877-7778. Sailboard and surfboard rentals, by the day or week; also variety of lessons.

Maui Windsurfari. 444 Hana Hwy., Kahului; (800) 736-6284/ *www.windsurfari.com*. Windsurf packages, with rental accommodations and car, and windsurfing equipment.

The Maui Windsurf Company. 22 Hana Hwy., Kahului; (808) 877-4816/(800) 872-0999/*www.mauiwindsurfcompany.com*. Offers complete windsurf packages, with accommodations, rental cars and all windsurfing equipment, from $539-$749.

Neil Pryde Maui. 400 Hana Hwy., Kahului; (808) 877-7443/(800) 321-7443/*www.neilprydemaui.com*. Windsurfing equipment sales.

Second Wind Sail and Surf. 111 Hana Hwy., Kahului; (808) 877-7467/(800) 936-7787/*www.secondwindmaui.com*. Windsurfing, kite boarding, surfing equipment rentals and sales. Full-service shop.

Surfing Schools

Goofy Foot Surf School. 505 Front St., Ste. 123, Lahaina; (808) 244-9283/*www.goofyfootsurfschool.com*. Offers small group and private lessons for beginners, as well as surf camps of various durations. All equipment provided. Lesson cost: $55.00-$125.00; surf camp cost: $250.00-$700.00.

Nancy Emerson School of Surfing. 505 Front St., Ste. 224B, Lahaina; (808) 244-7873/*www.mauisurfclinics.com*. Surf school specializing in instruction for beginners. Private and small group lessons; 1 hour to multi-day surf camps. Cost: $75.00-$1,750.00.

Parasailing

UFO Parasail. Whalers Village, Ka'anapali; (808) 661-7836. Offers rides of around 10 minutes in the air, $50-$60.

West Maui Parasail. Lahaina Harbor, Lahaina; (808) 661-4060/661-4887. Hour-long excursions, with rides of approximately 10 minutes in the air, for a distance of 400-800 feet. Cost: $53-$60.

Golf Courses

Kapalua Golf Club. At the Kapalua Bay Resort, Kapalua; (808) 669-8044/(877) 527-2582. The golf club has three notable courses—*The Plantation Course*, a newly-built, 18-hole, Ben Crenshaw-designed, situated on 250 acres, par 72 and 7,100 yards; and the 18-hole, Arnold Palmer-designed *Village* and *Bay* courses, both 72 par. Pro shop, driving range, club rentals, and restaurant on premises. Green fees (including cart): $250.00 ($100.00 twilight hours) at *The Plantation Course*; $200.00 ($95.00 twilight hours) at *The Bay Course*; and $185.00 ($85.00 twilight hours) at *The Village Course*.

Makena Golf Course. 5415 Makena Alanui, Makena; (808) 879-3344. Situated on 1,800 acres of undulating terrain. Offers two 18-hole, par-72, championship courses, the *North Course* and the 6,739-yard *South Course*, both designed by Robert Trent Jones, Jr. Green fees: $120.00 (including cart): $180.00 ($105 during twilight hours) at the *South Course*, and $170.00 ($95.00 twilight hours) at the *North Course*. Pro shop, driving range, and club rentals; also restaurant on premises.

Pukalani Country Club. 360 Pukalani, Pukalani; (808) 572-1314. 18-hole course; 6,570 yards, par 72. Green fees (including cart): $65.00 ($45.00 during twilight hours). Pro shop, driving range, club rentals, and restaurant.

Royal Ka'anapali Golf Courses. Located at the Ka'anapali Beach Resort, off Hwy. 30; (808) 661-3691. Offers two 18-hole, par-72, scenic courses along the coastline: the tournament *North Course*, designed by Robert Trent Jones, Jr., and the Jack Snyder-designed resort *South Course*. Green fees (including cart): $160.00 ($77.00 during twilight hours) at the *North Course*, and $130.00 ($65.00 during twilight hours) at the *South Course*. Pro shop, driving range, club rentals, and restaurant

Kahili Golf Course. 2500 Honoapi'ilani Hwy. (30), Waikapu; (808) 242-7090. Newly-built 18-hole course; 6,500 yards, par 72. Green fees (including cart): $80.00 ($60.00 twilight hours) . Facilities include a pro shop, driving range, and club rentals. Also restaurant on premises.

Elleair Golf Club. 1345 Pi'ilani Hwy.. Kihei; (808) 874-0777. 18-hole course; par 71, 6,801 yards. Green fees (including cart): $100.00 ($75.00 twilight hours). Pro shop, driving range, club rentals, restaurant.

Waiehu Municipal Golf Course. Off Kahekili Hwy. (340), Waiehu (2 miles north of Wailuku); (808) 243-7400. Oceanfront course; 18 holes, par 72. Green fees: $26.00 weekdays, $30.00 weekends; cart rental: $16.00. Pro shop, driving range, club rentals. Restaurant on premises.

Wailea Golf Courses. Wailea Alanui, Wailea; (808) 879-2966. There are three 18-hole, par-72, golf courses here, the first two designed by Jack Snyder and the third by Robert Trent Jones, Jr.—the challenging and scenic *Blue Course,* which features 42 lakes and 72 bunkers; the picturesque *Emerald Course,* with its abundant trees and lava rock: and the newly-built 7,000-yard, award-winning championship *Gold Course* which hosts the LPGA tournaments and Skins Games. Green fees (including cart): $185.00 at the *Gold Course* and the *Emerald Course*, and $175.00 at the *Blue Course*. Pro shop, and club rentals. Restaurant on premises.

MAUI | Tours and Activities

Tennis

Hyatt Regency Maui. 200 Nohea Kai Dr., Ka'anapali; (808) 661-1234, ext. 3174. Offers 5 hard courts. Pro shop, lessons. Court fee: $20.00.

Kapalua Tennis Garden. At the Kapalua Resort, 100 Kapalua Dr.. Kapalua; (808) 669-5677. 10 courts, including 4 lighted courts lor night play. Pro shop, lessons, rentals. Court fee: $15.00 per hour.

Makena Tennis Club. At the Maui Prince Hotel, 5400 Makena Alanui. Makena; (808) 879-8777. 6 courts. Lessons, rentals. Court fee: $28.00 per hour.

Maui Marriott Resort. 100 Nohea Kai Dr., Ka'anapali; (808) 667-1200. 5 courts, including 3 with lights. Pro shop, lessons, rentals. Court fee: $7.50 an hour, $6.00 for hotel guests.

Royal Lahaina Tennis Ranch. 2780 Keka'a Dr., Ka'anapali; (808) 661-3611, ext. 2296. 11 courts, including 6 lighted courts; also stadium court. Pro shop, lessons, rentals. Court fee: $10.00 per person, per day.

Sheraton Maui. 2605 Ka'anapali Pkwy., Ka'anapali; (808) 661-0031, ext. 5197. Offers 3 courts with lights. Pro shop, lessons, rentals. Court fee: $10.00 per person, per day; or $20.00 an hour.

Wailea Tennis Club. 131 Wailea Ike Place, Wailea; (808) 879-1958. Offers 11 championship hard courts, including 3 lighted courts for night play. Also 3 grass courts. Pro shop, rentals. Court fee: $12.00 per person, per day, with a minimum of 1 hour court time.

Public Tennis Courts. *Lahaina Civic Center,* Hwy. 30 (across from Wahikuli State Wayside Park), Lahaina; 2 courts with lights. *Malu-ulu-olele Park,* cnr. Front and Shaw Sts., Lahaina: 4 courts, with lights. *Kalama Park, S.* Kihei Rd. (½ mile south of mile marker 3), Kihei; 2 courts with lights. *Maui Community College,* cnr. Ka'ahumanu Ave. and Wakea Rd., Wailuku; 4 courts. *Wailuku War Memorial,* Ka'ahumanu Ave. (Hwy. 32), at mile marker 1, Wailuku; 4 lighted courts. *Hana Ball Park,* cnr. Hauoli St. and Uakea Rd., Hana; 2 courts with lights. *Eddie Tam Memorial Center,* Hwy. 377 (½ mile west of the intersection of Baldwin Ave.), Makawao; 2 courts, with lights. *Pukalani Community Center,* Pukalani St. (which goes off Haleakala Hwy., 37, midway between mile markers 6 and 7), Pukalani; 2 courts with lights.

Luaus

Drums of the Pacific Luau. At the Sunset Terrace at Hyatt Regency Maui, Ka'anapali; (808) 661-1234. All-you-can-eat buffets, featuring traditional Hawaiian dishes. Entertaining Polynesian shows. Luau dinners daily. Cost: $75.00 adults, $40.00 children; V.I.P. seating: $107 adults, $60.00 children. Reservations recommended.

Luau at Sheraton Maui. At the Sheraton Maui, Ka'anapali; (808) 661-0031. Beach front setting; Polynesian buffets. Entertainment features traditional songs and dances of Hawaii, Tahiti, Samoa and New Zealand. Luaus every night. Cost: $82.00 adults, $41.00 children; V.I.P. seating: $111.00 adults, $67.00 children. Reservations suggested.

Luau at Wailea Marriott. At the Wailea Marriott Resort, 3700 Wailea Alanui, Wailea; (808) 879-1922. Imu ceremony at sunset, followed by traditional Hawaiian buffet, and Polynesian revue. Luaus on Mon., Thurs. and Fri. Cost: $75.00 adults, $35.50 children. Reservations recommended.

Maui Marriott Luau. Held at the Maui Marriott, 100 Nohea Kai Dr., Ka'anapali; (808) 661-5828. Authentic Hawaiian luau; begins with a lei greeting ceremony, and features a buffet consisting of kalua pig, Hawaiian sweet potatoes and poi. Also Polynesian show, with songs and dances of the islands. Luaus every night (except Mon. and Sat.). Cost: $69.95 adults, $29.95 children; V.I.P. seating: $79.95 adults, $39.95 children. Reservations suggested.

Old Lahaina Luau. 505 Front St., Lahaina; (808) 667-1998/(800) 248-5828. Traditional Hawaiian buffet; features kalua roast pork, teriyaki steak, and mahi mahi, among other foods. Live music, and hula. Luaus daily. Cost: $85.00 adults, $55.00 children. Reservations recommended.

Royal Lahaina Luau. At the Luau Gardens at the Royal Lahaina Hotel, Ka'anapali; (808) 661-3611. Hawaiian and Polynesian foods. Live entertainment. Luaus offered every night (except Sat.). Cost: $77.00 adults, $40.00 children. Reservations recommended.

Wailea Renaissance Resort Luau. At the Renaissance Wailea Beach Resort, 3550 Wailea Alanui, Wailea; (808) 879-4900. Oceanfront setting. Luau begins with imu ceremony, followed by lavish Polynesian buffet. Also Polynesian show. Luau dinners on Wed. and Fri. Cost: $72.00 adults, $37.50 children. Reservations recommended.

Events on the Island

January

First Weekend. *Mercedes Championships*. Golf tournament, held at the Plantation Course at Kapalua Resort. World-class golfers compete for $5 million in prize money. For dates and more information, call (808) 669-2440/*www.kapalua.com*.

Second Weekend. *Maui Surf and Sand Half Marathon*. 13.1-mile half marathon, beginning at Kapalua at 320 feet and ending in downtown Lahaina. Also 5K run or walk. (530) 544-7095/*www.mauisurfsandhalf.com*.

Third Weekend. *Hula Fest Week*. Week-long, island-wide festival. Collegiate football all-star teams compete in the Hula Bowl Maui at the War Memorial Stadium in Wailuku. Also autograph sessions, Heisman Golf Tournament and a surf contest. More information at (808) 874-9500/*www.hulabowlmaui.com*. *Molokai Makahiki Festival*. At the Mitchell Pauole Community Center, Kaunakakai. Traditional Hawaiian festivities celebrating the period following the harvest; events include ceremonies, games, arts and crafts, and food concessions. More information at (808) 553-3673/*www.molokaievents.com*.

On-going. *Maui Arts and Cultural Center* in Kahului schedules various performing arts and music performances at the Castle Theater throughout the year. For a schedule, contact the center at (808) 242-7469/*www.mauiarts.org*.

February

First Weekend. *Wendy's Champions Skins Game*. Golf tournament at the Wailea Gold Course, Wailea Resort. Showcases professional and celebrity players. More information at (808) 875-7450/(800) 332-1614/*www.skinsgamesseries.com*.

Second Weekend. *Chinese New Year Celebration*. In downtown Lahaina. Two-day celebration of Chinese New Year, with traditional lion dances and parade on Front Street; also live music, demonstrations of Chinese martial arts, food booths, arts and crafts, calligraphy drawing, Chinese massage, games, and fireworks. Dates vary each year; more information at (888) 310-1117/*www.visitlahaina.com*.

Third Weekend. *Whale Day Celebration*. Kalama Park, Kihei. "Parade of Whales," celebrating the humpback whales that migrate here in the winter. Live entertainment and games, craft fair, food. (808) 249-8811/*www.greatmauiwhalefestival.com*.

March

Fourth Weekend. *Celebration of the Arts*. At the Ritz-Carlton, Kapalua. Premier Hawaiian arts and culture festival, celebrating the traditions and heritage of the Hawaiian people. More than 30 local artists offer hands-on lessons in traditional and contemporary Hawaiian art through workshops and demonstrations. Activities include films, music, lei making, kapa making, print making, and demonstration of Hawaiian nose flute; also food. (808) 669-6200/(800) 262-8440/*www.celebrationofthearts.org*. *Annual Haleakala Run to the Sun*. Popular annual event. The 36.2-mile marathon begins at the Maui Mall in Kahului, at sea level, and finishes at the top of Mt. Haleakala, at an elevation of 10,023 feet. More information at Valley Isle Road Runners, (808) 871-6441/*www.virr.com*.

April

First Weekend. *Annual East Maui Taro Festival*. Held at the Hana Ball Park in Hana. Festivities are centered around the Hawaiian staple, taro, and include exhibits, demonstrations and informative lectures. Also live band, hula, arts and crafts, Hawaiian voyaging canoes, farmers' market, visits to taro farms, taro pancake breakfast, Hawaiian food. More information at (808) 264-1553/*www.tarofestival.org*. *Hawaii Pro*. Held at Ho'okipa Beach Park in Paia. Prestigious wave windsurfing competition, drawing world-class windsurfers. 5-day event. More information at *www.pwaworldtour.com*.

Second Weekend. *Buddha Day*. Celebration of the birth of Buddha, with Buddhist festivities, including flower pageants, staged at Buddhist temples throughout the islands. For more information, call (808) 536-7044. *Art Maui*. At the Maui Arts and Cultural Center in Kahului. Multi-media event, featuring an exhibition of works of some 300 Maui artists. Exhibitions are staged throughout the month. More information at (808) 242-7469/*www.mauiarts.org*.

Third Weekend. *Annual Maui Scholastic Surf Championships*. At Ho'okipa Beach Park, Paia. Showcases some of the best high school surfers; competitions include shortboard, longboard and body board events. (808) 877-7111.

Fourth Weekend. *Banyan Tree Birthday Party*. Birthday bash for Lahaina's most famous landmark, the Banyan Tree. Displays and historical exhibits, including nature works from local artists; also arts and crafts for children, and a birthday cake. (888) 310-1117/*www.visitlahaina.com*. *Earth Day Celebration*. Hosted by Maui Nui Botanical Gardens, Kahului. Celebration of Earth Day in the Hawaiian tradition, with demonstrations in poi pounding, kapa beating and cordage making; also live entertainment, Hawaiian games, native plant sales, and food. For more information: (808) 249-2798/ *www.mnbg.org. Ulupalakua Thing (Maui County Agricultural Trade Show and Sampling).* At the Tedeschi Vineyards and Ulupalakua Ranch. One of Hawaii's oldest agricultural festivals, featuring local vendors showcasing Hawaiian agricultural products; also farmers' market, chefs' cooking competition and cooking demonstrations, and live entertainment. (808) 875-2839/(888) 808-1036/*www. ulupalakuathing.com.*

May

First Weekend. *The Fairmont Kea Lani May Day Celebration.* Celebration of Hawaiiana leis, held at the Fairmont Kea Lani in Wailea. Features arts and crafts, lei making and canoe paddling demonstrations, roaming hula dancers, and a May Day Court, complete with a king and queen in royal Hawaiian attire. Also live music. (808) 875-4100/*www.kealani.com.*

Second Weekend. *Kapalua Tennis Junior Vet/Senior Championship.* At the Kapalua Tennis Garden, Kapalua. Largest tennis tournament of its kind in the state, with matches scheduled for men and women 35 years and older. More information on (808) 669-5677/*www.kapaluamaui.com. Maui Classical Music Festival.* Long-running, week-long annual music festival, with world-famous musicians offering live performances at various locations across the island, including the Castle Theater in Kahului, Makawao and Hana. Concerts feature music of Mozart, Tchaikovsky, Chopin, Brahms, Mendelssohn, among others. (808) 879-4908/*www.maui-cmf.org.*

Third Weekend. *International Festival of Canoes.* Centered on Front Street, Lahaina. Two-week festival celebrating the art of canoe building: master carvers from across the Pacific congregate here to carve canoes from logs in the traditional ways, culminating in a parade on Front Street where the finished canoes are displayed. Also demonstrations in old-style surfboard building, drum making, Hawaiian house thatching, and other cultural Hawaiian arts. Daily arts and crafts fair in Banyan Tree Park on Front Street. (808) 667-9175/(888) 310-1117/*www.mauicanoefest.com.*

Fourth Weekend. *Barrio Fiesta.* Filipino cultural festival, held at the War Memorial Complex in Wailuku. Features arts and crafts, games, food, and the crowning of Miss Barrio. More information on (808) 244-3530.

June

Second Weekend. *Maui County Slalom Championships.* Windsurfing competitions held at Kanaha Beach Park, Kahului. For more information, call (808) 877-2111. *Annual Upcountry Fair.* Old-fashioned farm fair held at the Eddie Tam Center, Makawao. Live entertainment and agricultural exhibits. For more information, contact Maui Visitors Bureau (808) 244-3530/(800) 525-6284/*www. visitmaui.com.*

Third Weekend. *Kamehameha Day Celebration.* Annual celebration honoring Hawaii's first monarch, King Kamehameha I. Festivities held throughout the island. Colorful parade down Front Street in Lahaina, featuring floats, marching bands, and Pa'u riders on horses festooned with island flowers; also Hawaiian entertainment, food and arts and crafts in Lahaina's Banyan Tree Park. (888) 310-1117/*www.visitlahaina.com.*

July

First Weekend. *Old-Fashioned Fourth of July.* Front Street, Lahaina. Old-fashioned Independence Day celebration, with fireworks and a parade through downtown. Fireworks display begins at 8 p.m. (888) 310-1117/*www.visitlahaina.com. Bon Dance.* Jodo Mission, Lahaina. Buddhist ceremony honoring the souls of the dead. Festivities include a variety of games; also food concessions. For more information, call (808) 661-4304. *Makawao Rodeo.* Oskie Rice Arena, Makawao. Largest rodeo in the islands, with more than 300 contestants and $50,000 in prize money. Features 3 days of Western events, including horse races, bareback riding, roping, and country entertainment. Also parade through the town of Makawao. For a schedule of events and more information, call (808) 572-8102. *Wailea Open Tennis Tournament.* Held at the Wailea Tennis Club, Wailea. The event is part of the Grand Prix Tennis Tournament, open to Hawaii residents and USTA members. $10,000 in prizes. (808) 879-1958.

Second Weekend. *Kapalua Wine and Food Festival.* At the Kapalua Bay Hotel, Kapalua. Wine tasting, gourmet food, and panel discussions with wine and food experts. Includes sampling of reserve bottlings and also the Kapalua Seafood Festival. More information at (808) 669-2440/(866) 669-2440/*www.kapaluamaui.com.*

Fourth Weekend. *Maui County Slalom Race Championships.* Kanaha Beach Park, Kahului. Windsurfing slalom competitions, featuring windsurfers from around the world. For more information, call (808) 877-2111. *Hawaii International Jazz Festival.* Annual jazz festival that includes "Swingtime in Hawaii," held at the Maui Arts and Cultural Center. Features Hawaii's top jazz musicians. (808) 941-9974/(808) 242-7469/*www.hawaiijazz.com.*

August

First Weekend. *Maui Onion Festival.* Held at the Whaler's Village in Ka'anapali. Three-day celebration of the Maui onion, featuring a variety of food prepared with the famous sweet onions. Events include demonstrations by celebrity chefs, a recipe contest, a raw-onion-eating contest, a Maui onion and island produce open market, and arts and crafts and entertainment. (808) 661-4567/*www. whalersvillage.com*.

Second Weekend. *Hawaii State Slalom Championships.* Windsurfing competition, held at the Kanaha Beach Park near Kahului. Features some of Hawaii's best windsurfers. (808) 877-2111.

September

First Weekend. *Kapalua Open Tennis Tournament.* Held at the Kapalua Tennis Garden in Kapalua. Largest open tennis tournament in the state, with a prize of $10.000. Features some of Hawaii's top-seeded professional players. More information on (808) 669-0244/ *www.kapaluamaui.com*.

Second Weekend. *Hana Relay.* 52-mile relay race, with 6-person teams, from Kahului to Hana. Begins at the Kahului Airport and winds down the length of the scenic Hana Highway to end at the Hana Ball Park. For more information, contact Valley Isle Road Runners at (808) 871-6441/*www.virr.com*.

Third Weekend. *Taste of Lahaina.* At the Lahaina Recreation Park, Lahaina. This is Maui's largest culinary festival, in which some 25 local restaurants present cooking demonstrations and offer tastes of their signature dishes. Also wine tasting, beer garden, and live entertainment featuring some of Hawaii's best musicians. $5.00 admission fee; children free. More information at (888) 310-1117/ *www.visitlahaina.com*.

October

First Weekend. *Maui County Fair.* Held at the War Memorial Complex, Wailuku. Popular four-day event, drawing more than 90,000 people. Features a traditional fair with carnival rides, food concessions, games and entertainment, and livestock and other exhibits. (808) 270-7626.

Second Weekend. *Hula O Na Keiki Competition.* At the Ka'anapali Beach Hotel in Ka'anapali. Lively hula festival, with a variety of dance competitions, including individual competitions featuring young Hawaiian hula dancers. For more information, call (808) 661-0011/(800) 262-8450/*www.kbhmaui.com*.

Third Weekend. *Maui County Rodeo.* Held at the Oskie Rice Arena in Makawao. Two-day event, drawing real "paniolos"—Hawaiian cowboys—from throughout the island. Variety of Western events, including cow-roping competitions, bucking bulls, horse races, bareback riding and trick riding. For a schedule of events, call (808) 244-3530. *Aloha Week.* Week-long festival, with events staged throughout the island, at the Ka'anapali Beach Resort, Lahaina, Kihei, Wailea, Wailuku and Kahului. Features a variety of Hawaiian pageantry and demonstrations in lei making, poi pounding, coconut husking, coconut weaving and Hawaiian style of quilting. Also parades, arts and crafts, food, island fruit tasting, canoe races, and entertainment—including original Hawaiian music and hula dancers. For a schedule of events and more information, call (808) 878-1888/(808) 589-1771/*www.alohafestivals.com*.

Fourth Weekend. *Aloha Classic.* Held at Ho'okipa Beach Park, just east of Paia. 10-day event, comprising the Pro Windsurfing World Cup Final. Top windsurfers from 20 different countries compete for the $180,000 prize. More information on (808) 575-9151. *Halloween Parade.* Front Street, Lahaina. Includes a parade, costume contest, and a street party from 5 p.m. until midnight on the 31st. Also arts and crafts and food booths. More information at (888) 310-1117/*www.visitlahaina.com*.

November

Fourth Week. *Maui Invitational.* Pre-season NCAA basketball tournament, held at the Lahaina Civic Center in Lahaina, usually on Thanksgiving weekend. More information at (808) 661-4685.

December

First Weekend. *Na Mele O Maui Song Contest and Hula Festival.* Held at the Ka'anapali Beach Resort at Ka'anapali. Colorful festival of Hawaiiana; features arts and crafts shows, music, dance, and traditional Hawaiian song contests, including a children's singing competition; also, "Best of the Best" hula competition. More information at (808) 661-3271/(800) 245-9229/*www.kaanapali-resort.com*. *Maui Marathon.* 26-mile marathon, beginning at the Maui Mall in Kahului and ending at Whaler's Village, Ka'anapali. More than 300 runners participate. (808) 871-6441/*www.virr.com*. *Bodhi Day.* Traditional Buddhist celebrations at temples throughout the islands, marking the Buddhist Day of Enlightenment. For more information, call (808) 536-7044.

HAWAIIAN REEF FISH

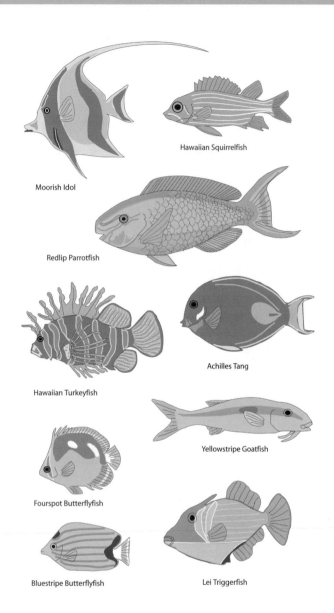

Moorish Idol

Hawaiian Squirrelfish

Redlip Parrotfish

Hawaiian Turkeyfish

Achilles Tang

Fourspot Butterflyfish

Yellowstripe Goatfish

Bluestripe Butterflyfish

Lei Triggerfish

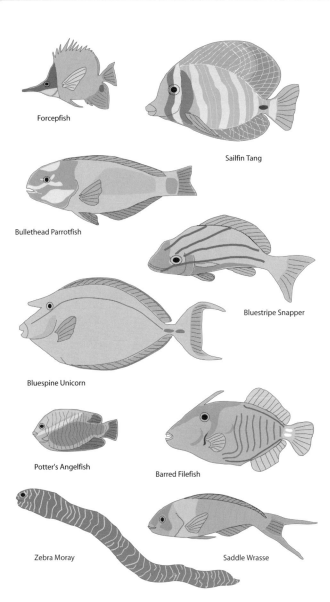

Forcepfish

Sailfin Tang

Bullethead Parrotfish

Bluestripe Snapper

Bluespine Unicorn

Potter's Angelfish

Barred Filefish

Zebra Moray

Saddle Wrasse

HAWAIIAN GAME FISH

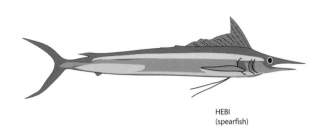

HEBI
(spearfish)

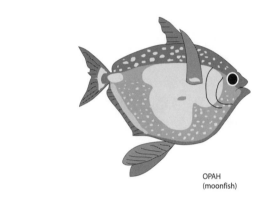

OPAH
(moonfish)

AHI
(yellowfin tuna)

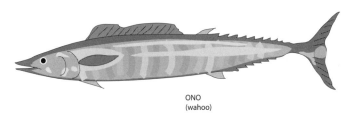

TOMBO
(albacore tuna)

ONO
(wahoo)

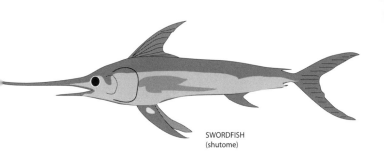

MAHI MAHI
(dolphin or dorado)

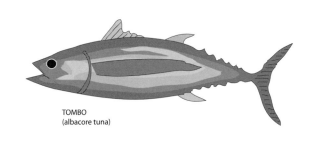

SWORDFISH
(shutome)

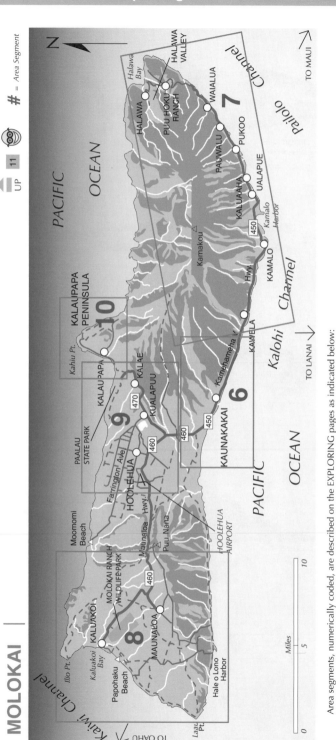

Area segments, numerically coded, are described on the EXPLORING pages as indicated below:

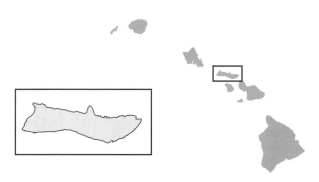

Molokai | Exploring the Island

Molokai may well be the most Hawaiian of the Hawaiian islands, and as far away from the rat race as you can get. It was one of Hawaii's first islands to be inhabited, yet, in the absence of any resort development and the "modernization" process that accompanies it, it remains largely in its natural state, with pristine rain forests, dry expanses of ranch land, and one of Hawaii's largest, most uncluttered beaches.

The island is 38 miles long and 10 miles wide, more or less slipper shaped. And like Maui it, too, is made up of two distinct, volcanic land masses, East Molokai and West Molokai, the first formed by Mount Kamakou, elevation 4,970 feet, and the second by Pu'u Nana, elevation 1,381 feet, joined together by a dry plain that makes up, at least for touring purposes, Central Molokai. East Molokai is the wet side of the island, and takes in virtually the entire segment of the island east of Molokai's principal town, Kaunakakai. West Molokai comprises, primarily, the arid slopes of Maunaloa that drop off onto a sandy, sun-baked coastline. An appendage at the north of the island, the Kalaupapa Peninsula, juts straight out into the ocean, beneath some of the tallest sea cliffs in the world, around 2,000 feet high.

For the purposes of exploring the island, we have divided Molokai into five geographically-grouped sections:

Kaunakakai, the island's principal town (which deserves a section of its own);

East Molokai, which takes in the southeast coast of the island, the 2,774-acre Kamakou Preserve and Halawa Valley;

West Molokai, made up of Maunaloa and a string of sandy beaches;

Central Molokai, which includes Ho'olehua and Pala'au State Park;

Kalaupapa Peninsula, the land mass at the north of the island.

[The numbers in the sidebar correspond to those in the number-coded map of the island.]

'MOLOKAI | Kaunakakai

Kaunakakai  *See Map 12 for Orientation* 6

Kaunakakai is Molokai's principal town, and an ideal base from which to explore the rest of the island. It is situated on the south coast of the island, some 7 miles southeast of the Molokai Airport in Ho'olehua, more or less equidistant from the remote east and west coasts of the island. It has in it most of the island's shops, restaurants and other amenities, including a handful of deli-cum-markets and local eateries, a gift shop, a sporting goods store, an art gallery, and even a bakery, the Kanemitsu Bakery—which sells freshly-baked "Molokai Bread"—all strung along a three-block section of the town's main street, Ala Malama. The town also offers some good accommodations—at the **Molokai Hotel**, a modest hotel with dining facilities, entertainment, and a swimming pool, situated just to the south of the Kamehameha V Highway (450), fronting on the ocean; and at the **Molokai Shores** condominiums, also oceanfront, situated just off the highway.

Kaunakakai is also notable for its harbor, the Kaunakakai Harbor—Molokai's only deep-water port—located just to the southwest of town, off Kaunakakai Road. The harbor originally provided a landing for early-day canoes, when native Hawaiians journeyed here for the plentiful fish found in the area. It is now a commercial port, where ferries and commuter boats to and from the neighboring island of Maui depart and arrive, and from where the island's honey, cattle, watermelons and other produce are shipped. The Kaunakakai Harbor is also home to fishing and charter boats, with some of them offering deep-sea fishing, diving, snorkeling, and even whale-watching excursions.

Kaunakakai also has its associations with King Kamehameha V, once the ruler of Hawaii, who maintained a **vacation home** here, the platform of which can still be seen near the beach on the west side of Kaunakakai Road, just above the wharf. Interestingly, the beach fronting the Kamehameha home site was once used exclusively by the *ali'i*—or chiefs—for sunbathing.

Of interest, too, a mile or so west of the center of Kaunakakai, off the highway (460), is **Kapuaiwa**, one of the last surviving royal coconut groves on the island, planted in the 1860s for Kamehameha V; and directly across from there, on the opposite side of the highway, is **Church Row**, with its small section of quaint, box-like churches—one for almost every denomination.

From Kaunakakai, Kamehameha V Highway (450) journeys east along the coast to the Halawa Valley, while Maunaloa Highway (460) heads out northwestward to the town of Maunaloa and farther to the remote west coast of the island. From Kaunakakai, too, you can explore Central Molokai, just to the north, or continue northward from there on Highways 460 and 470 to the sea cliffs above Kalaupapa.

MOLOKAI | Kaunakakai

= Point of Interest

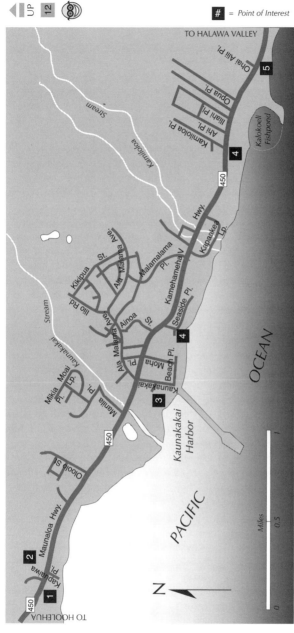

KAUNAKAKAI

1. Kapuaiwa
   Coconut Grove
2. Church Row
3. Kamehameha V
   Homesite
4. Molokai Shores
   Condominiums
5. Hotel Molokai

TO HALAWA VALLEY

Ohai Alii Pl.

Opua Pl.

Ilihi Pl.

Ahi Pl.

Kamiloloa Pl.

Stream

Kamiloloa

Kalokoeli
Fishpond

450 Hwy.

Kapaakea Lp.

Ala Malama Ave.

Malamalama Pl.

Kikipua St.

Kamehameha V

Ilio Rd

Stream

Kaunakakai

Ainoa St.

Seaside Pl.

OCEAN

Ala Malama Pl.

Moha Pl.

Beach Pl.

Kaunakakai

Mikia Moai Pl.

Manila Pl.

Kaunakakai
Harbor

450

Oloolo St.

PACIFIC

Maunaloa Hwy.

Kapuaiwa Pl.

Miles

0.5

N

TO HOOLEHUA

450

East Molokai   11 *See Map 11 for Orientation* 7

Kawela and Kamalo

East Molokai, for the purposes of our tour, comprises largely the area extending eastward from Kaunakakai, some 30 miles along the southeast coast of the island, to the Halawa Valley. The area was once the most densely populated on the island, dotted with more than 50 fishponds—an ancient form of Hawaiian aqua-culture—many of them dating from the 13th century, the remnants of some of which can still be seen along the coast here, mainly between Kaunakakai and Puko'o. Typically, a fishpond consisted of a narrow, encircling or straight wall, built from stone or coral, connecting two points of the shore, with small openings placed at intervals in the wall to allow the water to circulate. The pond was then stocked with fish, which were harvested as needed. A good example of this early form of Hawaiian ingenuity is the Kaloko'eli Fishpond, located directly behind the Molokai Shores condominiums, a little over a mile from the center of Kaunakakai. Another fishpond, easily viewed, is the Ali'i Fishpond, near the Oneali'i Beach Park, off the highway (450), some 3 miles from Kaunakakai.

In any event, East Molokai, besides its fishponds, has more to offer the visitor. Some 5 or 6 miles from Kaunakakai, for instance, eastward on the Kamehameha V Highway (450), lies **Kawela**, a small village, notable as the site of King Kamehameha I's invasion of Molokai in the late 1700s, in which Kamehameha defeated and conquered the island in his quest for domination over all the Hawaiian islands. At Kawela, just off the highway, are the Kakahai'a Beach Park and National Wildlife Refuge, the latter a sanctuary for rare endemic birds. Another place of note here is a *pu'ukaua*—or fortress—which served as a place of refuge for those escaping capture or death. The *pu'ukaua,* however, is situated in the deep Kawela Gulch, and is virtually inaccessible to visitors.

Another 4 miles or so—10 miles east of Kaunakakai—and we are at **Kamalo**, one of Molokai's few natural harbors, which, before the island's commerce was diverted to Kaunakakai, was an important landing spot for canoes and even small ships. At Kamalo you can also search out the small, wood-frame St. Joseph Church, built by Father Damien in 1876, located on the *makai* side of the highway, three-quarters of a mile past mile marker 10. There is a statue of Father Damien at the front of the church.

A mile or so past St. Joseph Church in Kamalo, alongside Highway 450, is the site of the Smith and Bronte Landing. Here, as students of aviation history will recall, on July 14, 1927, Ernest Smith and Emory Bronte crash-landed their airplane upon successful completion of their historic flight from California—the first civilian transpacific flight—which took all of 25½ hours. The site of the landing, now overgrown with brush and *kiawe* trees, is marked with a wooden sign.

Ualapu'e, Kalua'aha and Ili'iliopae Heiau

Farther still, another mile or so—at mile marker 13—lies the village of **Ualapu'e**, which has in it a general store and the ocean-front Wavecrest Condominiums, with rental units, a swimming pool and tennis courts; and one and one-half miles east of there is **Kalua'aha**, another small village, which, at one time, was the chief population center of Molokai. In Kalua'aha you can visit the Kalua'aha Church, the oldest Christian church on Molokai and, quite possibly, also one of the largest western-style churches in the islands. The church was built in 1844 by Reverend Harvey Hitchcock and his wife, who, incidentally, were the first Protestant missionaries to arrive in Kalua'aha.

Nearby, too, a little to the east of the Kalua'aha Church and also worth visiting, is Our Lady of Sorrows Church, built by Father Damien. The wood-frame church was originally built in 1874, and rebuilt in 1966.

Also of interest, three quarters of a mile farther, is the **Ili'iliopae Heiau**, Molokai's oldest and largest *heiau* (temple), reached by way of a foot trail which goes north off the highway briefly, crossing over a creek bed, to the base of the *heiau*. The *heiau*—which, according to local lore, was built in a single night by Hawaii's legendary *menehune* people who carried the stones for the building from the ocean near the Wailau Valley, some 7 miles over the mountains!—has an 87-foot-wide, 286-foot-long platform (believed to have originally been nearly 920 feet long). We must point out, however, that the *heiau* is located on private property and permission must be obtained through Molokai Visitors Association by calling (808) 553-3876; alternatively, you can arrange to tour the *heiau* with Molokai Trail and Wagon Ride (808-558-8380) who also tour the lush, surrounding countryside, including a visit to one of the world's largest mango groves.

In any case, the Ili'iliopae Heiau, besides being a place of worship, was once also a site for human sacrifices. Legend endures that a man once lived in the vicinity of the *heiau*, who had ten sons, nine of whom were sacrificed at the *heiau* by evil priests. Seeking to avenge the sacrifices, he sought out Kauhuhu, the shark god, who dwelled in a cave along Molokai's north coast. Kauhuhu agreed to avenge the deaths of the man's sons and sent a flood of water through the valley, destroying the *heiau* and washing the evil priests out to sea where, quite appropriately, they were eaten up by sharks

A little way from the Ili'iliopae Heiau, a half mile or so—some 16 miles east of Kaunakakai—lies Puko'o, which, during the 1900s, before the ascendancy of Kaunakakai as Molokai's commercial hub, was the seat of the island's government, with a court-house, jail, and a hotel located there. Puko'o is now a sleepy little village with only a small grocery store and snack bar. It is also the last place to replenish supplies before journeying farther east to the Halawa Valley.

Eastward still, some 4 miles, just before mile marker 20, on the *mauka*—inland—side of the highway, you can see the ruins of the Moanui Sugar Mill, originally built in the 1870s by plantation owner E. Baldwin, and destroyed by fire, some years later, in the 1880s; and just to the east of there, another quarter mile, at mile marker 20, is Murphey's Beach Park—a small, sandy beach, protected by a reef, which has good picnicking and swimming possibilities. The beach is named for George Murphey, former owner of the Pu'u O Hoku Ranch, who deeded the land for the park to the state. There are good views of Maui from here, across the Pailolo Channel, and also of Kanaha Rock and Moku Ho'oniki Island—both bird sanctuaries, and the latter also the site of a bombing range during World War II—just to the northeast.

A mile past Murphey's Beach, where the road turns sharply to the left around a huge rock, is Rock Point, one of Molokai's only surf breaks; and a little farther, past mile marker 22, after the highway begins to head inland, climbing northward, lies **Pu'u O Hoku Ranch**, with its green pastures dotted with grazing horses. This last, Pu'u O Hoku Ranch, was once owned by millionaire Paul Fagan, who later moved from Molokai to Hana, Maui, where he established the celebrated Hana Ranch. Interestingly, a famous prophet of Molokai, Lanikaula, is buried at Pu'u O Hoku Ranch in a sacred *kukui* grove. Lanikaula, we are told, lived on the eastern side of the island during the latter part of the 16th century, and his fame is largely derived from a momentous occasion when the king of Maui, Kamalalwalu, was preparing to invade the nearby island of Hawaii, and all the other prophets and priests offered the king flattering prophecies, except Lanikaula, who warned Kamalalwalu of imminent danger in the battle. Kamalalwalu, needless to say, was rather displeased with Lanikaula and vowed to kill him upon his return. However, as it turned out, Kamalalwalu was slain in battle on the Big Island of Hawaii, true to Lanikaula's prophecy, and his vow to put Lanikaula to death was left unfulfilled.

Halawa Valley

Beyond Pu' u O Hoku Ranch, the highway begins its descent into the lush, green Halawa Valley, passing by an overlook, roughly a mile past mile marker 25, from where you can see the picturesque Moa'ula and Hipuapua falls cascading hundreds of feet down the verdant hills above the valley; and a mile farther—some 27 miles east of Kaunakakai—the highway (450) finally ends in Halawa Valley. Halawa Valley is notably the site of the first recorded settlement on Molokai, dating from 650 A.D. It was once inhabited by hundreds of families and covered with *taro* patches, supplying much of the island with *taro,* the Hawaiian staple. Even as late as 1836, the population of Halawa Valley was around 500. However, in 1946, a *tsunami* (tidal wave) devoured much of the valley, engulfing farms and dwellings alike, and in the following years only a handful of families returned to live in the valley.

In Halawa Valley itself, at the end of the highway lies Halawa Beach Park, situated along Halawa Bay at the mouth of the Halawa River and frequented mainly by fishermen and some vacationing families. Interestingly, Halawa Bay was once also a well-regarded spot for surfing, where the island's chiefs practiced the sport. It continues to attract dedicated surfers to this day.

At any rate, among Halawa Valley's chief attractions are the Moa'ula and Hipuapua waterfalls, 250 feet and 500 feet high, respectively. The first of these, the Moa'ula Falls, can be reached by way of a 2½-mile trail that dashes off the highway (450) westward, roughly a quarter mile south of **Halawa Beach Park**, passing by rows of banana, papaya and guava trees. A quarter mile or so from the highway turnoff, the trail crosses over two streams and heads north, alongside another freshwater stream, some 2 miles to the foot of the waterfalls, where there is a refreshing, natural pool, ideal for swimming. But a word of caution: in this icy pool, according to ancient legend, lives a *mo'o*—or lizard—and visitors must seek its permission before plunging in: drop a *ti* leaf into the pool, and if the leaf floats, you may enjoy the pool without further ado; if not, beware, danger lurks!

There are also trails leading to the Upper Moa'ula and Hipuapua falls, more difficult than the Moa'ula Falls trail, but well worth the effort, especially for outdoor enthusiasts. Both trails branch off the Moa'ula Falls trail, a hundred yards or so before reaching the Moa'ula Falls. We must point out, though, that the Upper Moa'ula Falls trail, which goes west off the Moa'ula Falls trail, is especially treacherous, narrowing at one point to a mere ledge along a sheer mountainside, with only a cable—bolted to the side of the mountain—for support. In any case, the pool at the base of the waterfalls offers a degree of solitude unattainable elsewhere, with picnicking and swimming possibilities to boot. There are also spectacular views of the valley below, tumbling down toward the ocean.

The Hipuapua Falls trail is not quite as difficult or hair-raising as the one leading to the Upper Moa'ula Falls, but neither is it easy to find, covered with rocks and foliage and seldom trodden. But for the persevering sort, we suggest hiking down from the Moa'ula Falls trail, past the Upper Moa'ula Falls trail turnoff, to the Hipuapua Stream and following it upstream more or less directly to the falls. The Hipuapua Falls are magnificent, 500-foot waterfalls, where few, if any, venture, leaving it for the fortunate handful to enjoy.

MOLOKAI | East Molokai

Waikolu Lookout and Kamakou Preserve

There remains yet another area to explore in East Molokai. Northwestward from Kaunakakai on Highway 460, some 4 miles, the rugged Maunahui Road—the main forest road—dashes off into the wild, mountainous terrain to the east, climbing more than 3,000 feet to the **Waikolu Lookout**, and passing by, some 9 miles from the highway turnoff, Lua Na Moku 'Iliahi—the Sandalwood Measuring Pit—where you can still see the eroded pit in the clearing, originally dug out in the 1800s to duplicate, in shape and size, a ship's hold. Interestingly, during the days of the sandalwood trade the pit was used as a measure: it would be filled with sandalwood logs, representing a ship's load, and at the end of negotiations between the island's chiefs and the ships' captains, the sandalwood would be transferred to the ships waiting just off shore

In any case, a mile or so past the Sandalwood Measuring Pit is the Wailoku Lookout, at an elevation of 3,700 feet, from where you can see the lush, amphitheater-like Wailoku Valley, frequently rain-soaked and dotted with waterfalls and streams. From the Wailoku Valley, a 5½-mile water tunnel, bored through the valley itself, channels rainwater into the Kualapu'u Reservoir at Kualapu'u. At the Wailoku Lookout, too, there is a grassy picnic area with some camping possibilities.

Finally, just to the east of the Wailoku Lookout lies the expansive, 2,774-acre **Kamakou Preserve**, which has in it, more or less at its center, the lofty Mt. Kamakou, the highest peak on Molokai, at an elevation of 4,970 feet. The Kamakou Preserve, originally established in 1982 by the Nature Conservancy of Hawaii, is a nature wonderland of sorts, filled with rain forests and lush, rain-soaked valleys, and home to no fewer than five endangered species of birds, including two that are found only on Molokai: the Molokai Creeper and Molokai Thrush. There are several species of native Hawaiian plants and ferns here as well, and groves of rare Hawaiian sandalwood trees. Besides which, the area has a fair number of hiking trails, meandering, quite enchantingly, through the lush wilderness. It is, however, a good idea to contact the Nature Conservancy of Hawaii, at (808) 553-5236, for current information on the trails before striking out on foot into the misty wilderness.

West Molokai

  See Map 11 for Orientation

Maunaloa

West Molokai lies largely between the 1,381-foot Pu'u Nana peak and the ocean, on the slopes of the volcanic Maunaloa mountain. It comprises, for the most part, dry, arid land, with Maunaloa, situated more or less in the center of West Molokai, as its principal town. Maunaloa is also notable as the birthplace of the *hula,* the traditional Hawaiian dance of storytelling. It was here, according to local lore, that the goddess Laka learned the art of the *hula* from her sister, Kapo, then traveled to all the other islands, teaching the public this traditional Hawaiian dance.

Maunaloa itself is a small, rustic, one-street, former plantation town, located some 17 miles west of Kaunakakai at the end of Maunaloa Highway (460), and built in 1923 by Libby, McNeil & Libby to house the company's pineapple plantation workers. The town has a general store, one or two eateries, and a handful of little shops, notable among them the **Big Wind Kite Factory**. This last, situated approximately at the center of town, has on display a color-ful assortment of handcrafted kites, and its staff offer factory tours as well as kite flying lessons.

Also at Maunaloa, situated some 1,200 feet above the ocean on a 65,000-acre spread owned by the Molokai Ranch Company—the island's largest landholder—is **The Lodge at Molokai Ranch**, a 22-room, two-story hotel that offers perhaps the island's only luxury accommodations, with all the modern conveniences and a heated pool and an elegant dining facility on its premises. Molokai Ranch also owns and operates the nearby oceanfront Beach Village that fronts on Kaupoa Beach and offers more primitive accommodations in two-bedroom canvas "tentalows" on platform decks, with open-air conveniences.

West Molokai Beaches

Some 4 miles or so northwest of the Maunaloa township on Kalua-koi Road—which actually goes off Maunaloa Highway (450)—is Kaluakoi, a tiny community situated at the head of Kaluakoi Bay, along a stretch of white-sand beach known as Kepuhi Beach, on the island's northwest shore. Once home to the Sheraton Molokai—which later became the Kaluakoi Hotel, now defunct—has in it a couple of condominium developments, Ke Nani and Paniolo Hale, as well as the oceanfront, 18-hole, championship Kaluakoi Golf Course.

Also at Kaluakoi, just to the south of Kepuhi Beach and separated from it by Kaiak Rock, a 110-foot cinder cone, is **Papohaku Beach**, one of Hawaii's largest white-sand beaches, some 3 miles long and, at places, nearly a hundred yards wide, bordered by *kiawe* trees. There are three access points to Papohaku Beach: the first, off Kaluakoi Road, a mile or so south of the old Kaluakoi Hotel, leads to a developed beach park with showers and restrooms and some camping possibilities; the second, a little over a half-mile farther to the south, is by way of Lauhue Road, which goes off Kaluakoi Road; and the last, another three-quarters of a mile southward, is off Kulua Road, which goes off Papapa Place, which, in turn, goes off Kaluakoi Road. These last two beach accesses lead to essentially undeveloped beach parks, with the latter bordered by rocky outcroppings at its southern end, where Papohaku Beach finally ends.

There are other beaches along the coast here as well. Some 2 miles or so south from Papohaku Beach—reached on Kaluakoi Road and Poha Kuloa Road—lies Kapukahehu Beach, popularly known as "Dixie Maru Beach," named for the *Dixie Maru,* a sampan that wrecked just off the rocky coast here in the 1920s. The beach itself is small, crescent-shaped, and sandy, with good swimming possibilities.

Another beach here, north of Kepuhi Beach, is Pohaku Mauliuli Beach, a small, secluded, crescent-shaped white-sand beach, also known as Make Horse—or "Dead Horse"—Beach, evidently named for the fact that a horse once fell off a cliff here and died. The beach, nevertheless, is an excellent place for picnicking, although swimming is not encouraged due to the strong ocean currents, making it rather unsafe for the sport. The beach can be reached by way of Kaluakoi Road, some 4½ miles from the Highway 450 intersection, then Kaka'ako Road northward—at the Paniolo Hale Condominiums—another quarter mile, and Leo Place west off Kaka'ako Road a half mile or so, directly to the beach.

Also try to visit Kawakiu Beach, situated at the head of Kawakiu Nui Bay, a half mile or so north of Pohaku Mauliuli Beach (Make Horse Beach), and reached on Kaluakoi Road northwest from Highway 450, then Kaka'ako Road directly northward until the paved portion of the road ends, from where a dirt trail leads another half mile or so to the beach. Interestingly, beginning in 1952, Kawakiu Beach was also the starting point for the celebrated Molokai-to-Oahu Canoe Race for several years, until in 1963 the race was finally moved to the Hale O Lono Harbor along the southwest coast of the island. Also, in 1975, Kawakiu Beach was the scene of a peaceful demonstration by the Hui Alaloa—a group of Hawaiian activists—demanding public access to the beach, which was then granted by the Molokai Ranch Company. The beach, in any case, is one of Molokai's most beautiful—sandy, secluded, and with excellent swimming possibilities during the summer months. It is also a good place for snorkeling during calm seas, especially along the northern end of the cove, with its crystal clear waters and abundant coral.

9

Central Molokai

See Map 11 for Orientation

Central Molokai comprises primarily the vast dry plain connecting the island's two land masses, East Molokai and West Molokai. At the heart of it lies **Ho'olehua**, a small town with only a post office, but with the Ho'olehua Airport located just to the southwest of it. The town is surrounded by 40-acre parcels of agricultural land that were made available to native Hawaiians, beginning in 1932, by the Hawaiian Homes Commission. Ho'olehua also has one or two places of visitor interest quite close to it. Just to its west, for instance, about a mile from Highway 470 on Farrington Avenue westward, then northwestward on Lihi Pali Avenue another half-mile or so, is **Purdy's Macadamia Nut Farm**, one of the island's foremost attractions. Purdy's is situated on a 1½-acre Hawaiian homestead, with a 60-year-old grove of some 45 macadamia nut trees. Here you can tour the orchard as well as learn all about the nuts—how they are grown, harvested and processed, all naturally. You can also sample the nuts, both raw and roasted, and also coconuts and macadamia nuts honey.

Also of interest, some 3½ miles northwest of Ho'olehua—reached on Farrington Avenue and Mo'omomi Road northwestward, then a short walk west along the shoreline—is the Mo'omomi Beach area, a stretch of mostly undeveloped beaches, bordering on Mo'omomi Bay and frequented primarily by fishermen. The Mo'omomi Beach area offers some beachcombing possibilities, although swimming and sunbathing are not recommended due to unsafe ocean conditions and strong afternoon tradewinds. However, some 2 miles to the west of Mo'omomi Bay you can visit the island's only sand dunes at a remote area known as Keonelele, or "flying sands, frequently also referred to as the "Desert Strip."

Yet another place of interest, situated just to the east of Ho'olehua at the intersection of Highways 470 and 480, is Kualapu'u, a small town with a plantation-era, grid-style layout, which has on its outskirts the world's largest rubber-lined reservoir—with a water capacity of 1.4 billion gallons!—built in the 1960s to supply water to central and west Molokai. In Kualapu'u itself there are a market, restaurant and service station.

Some 2½ miles northwest from Kualapu'u on Highway 470, sits the village of Kalae, which has in it the **R.W. Meyers Sugar Mill**, an authentically restored mill. The mill was originally built in 1878 by Rudolf W. Meyers, a German immigrant who arrived in Molokai in 1850, married the high chieftainess, Kalama Waha, and had eleven children by her. Meyers managed the Molokai Ranch lands for King Kamehameha V, as well as the Kalaupapa settlement just to the north, and successfully operated his sugar mill from 1878 until 1889. At the mill you can learn all about sugar production—from the crushing of the sugarcane to the heating, evaporating and cooling processes that produce a crystallized form of sugar and molasses, which is then placed in a centrifuge (powered by a steam engine), thus separating the molasses from the final product—raw sugar. The mill museum also has several artifacts on display, centered, again, on sugar production. The mill is open to the public daily, 10 a.m.-12 noon.

North from the Meyers Sugar Mill, roughly a mile on Highway 470, lies the **Pala'au State Park**, a splendid 234-acre park, situated at an elevation of approximately 1,600 feet. The park has in it forests of ironwood and eucalyptus, and good, abundant opportunities for picnicking and hiking. At the park you can also visit the **Kalaupapa Lookout**, which has commanding views of the Kalaupapa Peninsula below, as well as interpretive displays identifying and describing the various landmarks on the peninsula, among them the old lighthouse, built in 1909, at the northern tip of the peninsula, and the Kalaupapa settlement, the Kalaupapa Airfield, and the Kauhako Crater at the southeast end of the peninsula. From here it is also easy to see how the 2,000-foot-high cliffs formed a natural barrier between Kalaupapa and the rest of Molokai. Near the park, too, are the Molokai Mule Ride stables, from where you can take a mule ride down to the Kalaupapa Peninsula, descending nearly 1,600 feet, zig-zagging along a narrow, 3-mile trail with some 26 switchbacks.

Also at the Pala'au State Park, a trail leads through ironwood groves to Kaule O Nanahoa—or **Phallic Rock**—which, in many ways, resembles the male organ. Interestingly, Phallic Rock has its associations with a man named Nanahoa and his wife, Kawahuna, who, we are told, lived on this hill a long, long time ago. One day, according to legend, Nanahoa gazed and smiled upon a beautiful young girl who was looking at her reflection in a pool of water nearby. Kawahuna, quite understandably, became jealous, and grabbed the young girl by her hair. At which point, Nanahoa, outraged by his wife's actions, struck her in anger and sent her tumbling down the hillside, where she turned into stone. As it turned out, though, Nanahoa was also turned into stone, albeit in the form of a phallus—hence the name, Phallic Rock. The rock, as locals will tell you, is now bestowed with magical powers of fertility, where childless women have spent the night and returned home, soon to conceive.

Kalaupapa   See Map 13 for Orientation **10**

The Kalaupapa Peninsula is situated along the central part of Molokai's rugged north shore, surrounded on three sides by ocean and on the fourth by 2,000-foot-high sea cliffs—the highest in the world. The peninsula itself was created by the Kauhako volcano, the crater of which can be seen at the southeast end of the peninsular tract.

The Kalaupapa Peninsula is best-known as the site of Hawaii's infamous leper colony. Beginning in 1866, victims of the disease of leprosy were banished by the Hawaiian monarchy to this desolate corner of the island—a natural prison. All too frequently, the afflicted were taken from their families and transported by ship to Kalawao, on the eastern side of the peninsula, where they were thrown overboard and left to fend for themselves. In 1873, however, Father Damien de Veuster, a Belgian priest, arrived at Kalaupapa and devoted himself to the care of the lepers who, until then, had lived in great misery, without adequate food or shelter; but in 1884, he, too, contracted the disease, and five years later, in 1889, he died at the age of 49. Father Damien's good work was nevertheless continued by Mother Marianne, who arrived at Kalaupapa in 1888, and lived and worked here tirelessly for the next 30 years, improving the health and living conditions of the patients at Kalaupapa, until her death at the age of 80. By the 1940s, of course, the discovery and introduction of sulfone drugs had rendered leprosy—or Hansen's Disease, as it had come to be known—a curable disease that was no longer contagious, and some years later, the inhabitants of Kalaupapa were cured and free to leave at their choosing. Most, however, chose to stay, for Kalaupapa was the only home they had known for much of their lives.

Kalaupapa is now a National Historical Park, but one where the public is not permitted to wander unsupervised, as some 80 former patients still live there. Visitors, nevertheless, can take guided van tours of the settlement and the peninsula, taking in the Kalaupapa grounds and buildings, including a 1900s store and one or two dispensaries, as well as the white, steepled **St. Philomena Church**, [6] built by Father Damien in 1872. On the tour you can also see other churches—Catholic, Protestant, Mormon—mostly dating from the 19th century, and visit the grassy Kalawao Park on the east side of the peninsula, overlooking the ocean and the north coast of the island. Also on the tour is a stop at the Kalaupapa museum-cum-bookstore, which has old photos recounting the history of Kalaupapa and its inhabitants, and books on Father Damien, Mother Marianne, and Kalaupapa.

Kalaupapa can be reached either on foot by hiking down from the Pala'au State Park some 1,600 feet—which takes approximately an hour down to the peninsula and one and one-half hours back up—or on a scheduled flight directly to the **Kalaupapa Airfield**. [4]

UP 13

= Point of Interest

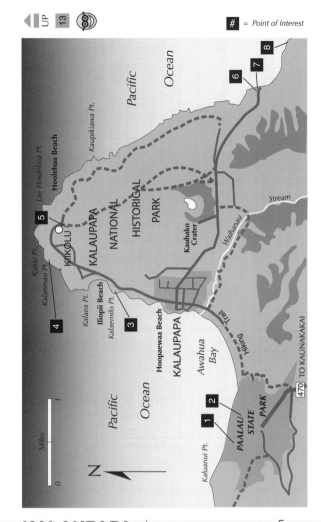

KALAUPAPA PENINSULA

1. Kalaupapa Overlook
2. Phallic Rock
3. Ocean View Pavilion
4. Kalaupapa Airfield
5. Molokai Lighthouse
6. St. Philomena Church
7. Father Damien Monument
8. Judd Park

Accommodations | Molokai

Kamalo Plantation and Moanui Beach House. *$150.00.* P.O. 300, Kaunakakai, HI 96748; (808) 558-8236. 2-bedroom, 1½-bathroom house with open lanais, overlooking the ocean. Fully equipped with cooking appliances, barbecue grill, TV, VCR, radio; also ocean kayaks. Complimentary fresh tropical fruit basket. 3-night minimum stay.

Paniolo Hale. $95-$160. Kaluakoi Rd. (off Hwy. 460), Maunaloa; (800) 367-2984. 39 condominium units, with TV, phones, ceiling fans, and kitchens; also private lanais with hot tubs. Swimming pool, and paddle court. Weekly maid service. Minimum stay: 3 nights.

Hotel Molokai. *$90-$175.* Kamehameha V Hwy. (450), Kaunakakai;

(808) 553-5347/(800) 535-0085/*www.hotelmolokai.com*. 55 oceanfront units with private baths and lanais. Swimming pool, restaurant and cocktail lounge on premises.

Kaluakoi Villas. *$140-$250.* Kepuhui Beach, Maunaloa; (808) 545-3510/(800) 367-5004/*www.castleresorts.com*. 300-unit beach front condominium complex with studios and 1-bedroom units. TV, phones; swimming, restaurant and cocktail lounge.

Ke Nani Kai. $105-$150. P.O. Box 289, Maunaloa, HI 96770; (808) 552-2761/(800) 888-2791. 120 one- and two-bedroom condominium units in West Molokai, with TV and phones; some ocean views. Also swimming pool, and tennis courts. Located adjacent to Kaluakoi Golf Course.

Molokai Shores. $85-$125. Kamehameha V Hwy. (450), Kaunakakai; (808) 553-59547(800) 535-0085. 42 1- and 2-bedroom units in oceanfront condominium complex. TV, and kitchens. Also swimming pool, putting green and barbecue area.

Wavecrest Resort. *$175-$330.* Star Route 155, Kaunakakai; (808) 553-3666/(800) 600-4158/*www.molokairealty.com*. Ocean-front condominium complex with 21 units with TV and kitchens, located 13 miles east of Kaunakakai. Swimming pool and tennis courts on premises. Minimum stay, 3 nights.

The Lodge & Beach Village at Molokai Ranch. *$148-$430.*100 Maunaloa Hwy., Maunaloa; (808) 660-2824/(888) 627-8082/*www. molokairanch.com*. Small, luxury resort on 65,000 acres, with two distinct lodging properties: the 22-room Lodge, situated at an elevation of 1,200 feet, overlooking the ocean; and the 40-unit oceanfront Beach Village. The Lodge offers rooms with wet bars, refrigerators, TVs, and data ports; the village has 2-bedroom canvas "tentalows" with open-air conveniences. Swimming pool, restaurant and lounge at The Lodge. Also 18-hole golf course nearby.

Molokai Beach House. *$250.* (808) 599-3838/(888) 575-9400/

www.molokaibeachhouse.com. 3-bedroom, 2-bathroom oceanfront house on Molokai's east shore, 2 miles from pristine Halawa Valley. Fully furnished, with linen, appliances, cable and internet connections. Also picnic table, hammock by the ocean. Minimum stay: 3 nights.

Dining | Molokai

[Restaurant prices—based on full-course dinner, excluding drinks, lax and tips—are categorized as follows: *Deluxe*, over $30; *Expensive*. $20-$30; *Moderate*. $ 10-$20; *Inexpensive*, under $ 10.]

Hula Shores. *Moderate.* At the Hotel Molokai, Kamehameha V Hwy. (450), Kaunakakai; (808) 553-5347. Open-air setting; overlooking the ocean, with views of Lanai. Fresh local seafood, steaks, and poultry dishes; also salad bar. Entertainment. Open for breakfast, lunch and dinner daily. Reservations recommended

Kanemitsu Bakery & Restaurant. *Inexpensive.* Ala Malama, Kaunakakai; (808) 553-5855. Famous for its freshly-baked "Molokai Bread." Also burgers and plate lunches. Open for breakfast, lunch and dinner daily (except Tues.).

Maunaloa Room. *Moderate.* At the Molokai Ranch, 100 Maunaloa Hwy., Maunaloa; (808) 627-8082/(888) 627-8082/www. molokairanch.com. Ocean view restaurant with wrap-around verandahs; indoor and outdoor seating. Serves Molokai regional cuisine prepared with fresh, local ingredients. Menu features Eggs Maunaloa, a signature dish, and fresh island mahi-mahi served with pineapple chutney and sesame rice. Open for breakfast and dinner. Reservations suggested.

Molokai Drive Inn. *Inexpensive.* Kaunakakai; (808) 553-5655. Hamburgers, hot dogs, chili and salads: also chicken slew, shrimp, fried saimin, and ice cream. Plate lunches. Open for lunch and dinner daily.

Outpost Natural Foods. *Inexpensive.* Kaunakakai; (808) 553-3377. Offers a variety of natural foods, including sandwiches, burritos and fruit smoothies. Open 10 a.m.-6 p.m. daily.

Oviedo's Lunch Counter. *Inexpensive.* Puali Rd., Kaunakakai; (808) 553-5014. Home-style Filipino food. House specialty is pork adobo. Open 10 a.m.-5 p.m. daily.

THINGS TO SEE AND DO

Places to See | Points of Interest at a Glance

Big Wind Kite Factory. 120 Maunaloa Hwy., Maunaloa; (808) 552-2364/*www.molokai.com/kites*. Unique specialty store, offering an assortment of colorful, handcrafted kites and windsocks; also kite flying lessons, and factory tours. Open 8.30-5.00 daily.

Halawa Valley. Located at the east end of the island, approximately 27 miles from Kaunakakai, reached more or less directly on Kamehameha V Hwy. (450). Lush, green valley, site of the first recorded settlement on Molokai, dating from 650 A.D. The valley has in it, as its chief attractions, the *Halawa Beach Park*, situated along Halawa Bay, at the mouth of the Halawa River; and the *Moa'ula* and *Hipuapua* waterfalls, 250 feet and 500 feet, respectively, located farther upriver. The Moa'ula Falls can be reached by way of a rugged, 2½-mile hiking trail that goes off the highway (450), roughly a quarter mile south of Halawa Beach Park; and the Hipuapua Falls Trail branches off the Moa'ula Falls trail, just before reaching the Moa'ula Falls. There is also a rather difficult trail leading to the Upper Moa'ula Falls, which, too, branches off the Moa'ula Falls trail, a hundred yards or so before reaching the latter.

Ili'iliopae Heiau. Located off Kamehameha V Hwy. (450), approximately 15½ miles of Kaunakakai; reached by way of a dirt road which goes north off the highway, a ½ mile past mile marker 15, then onto the Wailau Trail which leads directly to the *heiau*. The *heiau* is on private property; permission to visit the *heiau* may be obtained from *Molokai Visitors Association*, (808) 553-3876, or *Molokai Trail and Wagon Rifle*, (808) 558-8380. The Ili'iliopae Heiau is Molokai's oldest and largest *heiau*, with an 87-foot-wide and 286-foot-long platform, which is originally believed to have been 920 feet long. In ancient times, the *heiau* was both a place of worship and human sacrifice.

Kalaupapa Peninsula. Situated on Molokai's remote north shore, beneath 2,000-foot-high cliffs, and reached by way of a steep, narrow 3-mile hiking trail with 26 switchbacks, or by air. The peninsula itself, isolated from the rest of the island, was once the site of a leper colony, established in 1866 and finally abandoned in the 1940s. It is now preserved as the *Kalaupapa National Historical Park,* with tours of the area available to visitors. Tours take in the Kalaupapa settlement and its buildings, including a 1900s store, one or two dispensaries, the white, steepled St. Philomena Church, built by Father Damien in 1872, and the 19th-century Catholic, Protestant and Mormon churches. Also included on the tour are a visit to the Kalawao Park, on the east side of the peninsula, and the Kalaupapa

museum-cum-bookstore, which has old photos recounting the
history of Kalaupapa and its inhabitants, as well as books on Father
Damien, Mother Marianne, and Kalaupapa. For touring information and visitor permits (which are required to visit the peninsula),
contact *Father Damien Tours* at (808) 567-6171.

Kamakou Preserve. Northeast of Kaunakakai, approximately 8
miles; reached by way of Hwy. 460 northwestward some 4 miles,
then the mountainous Maunahui Rd. directly east another 8 miles
to the reserve. Large, 2,774-acre preserve, which has in it Mt.
Kamakou, the highest peak on the island, at an elevation of 4,970
feet. The park itself is a nature wonderland of sorts, filled with rainforests and lush valleys, and home to at least five endangered species of birds, including the Molokai Creeper and Molokai Thrush.
The park also has in it several species of native Hawaiian plants and
ferns, and some groves of rare Hawaiian sandalwood trees. Good
hiking possibilities; for wilderness trail information, contact the
Nature Conservancy of Hawaii, at (808) 553-5236.

Pala'au State Park. At the end of Kalae Hwy. (470), approximately a mile north of Kalae (or 3½ miles northeast of Ho'olehua).
234-acre state park, at an elevation of 1,600 feet, overlooking the
Kalaupapa Peninsula. Good picnicking and hiking possibilities,
with trails leading through groves of ironwood and eucalyptus, to
the Kalaupapa Lookout and the legendary Phallic Rock. The park is
open to the public daily.

Purdy's Natural Macadamia Nut Farm. Located off Lihi Pali Ave.
(which goes off Farrington Ave., which, in turn, goes off Hwy. 470),
in Ho'olehua; (808) 567-6601. This is one of Molokai's foremost
attractions, situated on a 1½-acre Hawaiian homestead, with a
60-year-old grove of some 45 macadamia nut trees. Tours of the
orchard are offered, explaining all about the nuts—how they are
grown, harvested and processed, all naturally, Also sampling of
nuts, both raw and roasted, as well as delicious coconut and macadamia honey. Open Tue.-Fri. 9.30-3.30, Sat. 10-2. Free admission.

R. W. Meyer Sugar Mill. Located on Hwy. 470, 4 miles north
of intersection of Hwy. 460, in Kalae; (808) 567-6436. Authentically restored sugar mill, originally built in 1878. Now a museum
and cultural center, featuring several artifacts of interest, centered
around the sugar industry. Also exhibits and tours describing the
entire sugar-making process. Open 10-2, Mon.-Sat. Admission fee:
$2.00.

Places to Go | Beaches

Halawa Beach Park. At the end of Kamehameha V Hwy. (450), approximately 27 miles east of Kaunakakai. The beach park is situated along Halawa Bay and is generally safe for swimming, except during high tide. Popular with surfers and fishermen. Facilities include a pavilion, barbecue grills, and restrooms.

Kapukahehu Beach (Dixie Maru Beach). Located 2 miles south of Popohaku Beach, at the end of Poha Kuloa Rd. which goes off Kaluakoi Rd., at its southwestern end. Small, crescent-shaped sandy beach. Offers safe swimming conditions, except during high surf.

Kawakiu Beach. Situated on Kawakiu Nui Bay; reached by way of a dirt trail that goes off Kaka'ako Rd. (which goes off Kaluakoi Rd.), at the very end, near the 14th green of Kaluakoi Golf Course, passing through arid stretches overgrown with kiawe trees. Lovely, secluded, crescent-shaped, sandy beach. Swimming not advised during the winter and spring months.

Kepuhi Beach. Situated off Kaika Rd., which goes off Kaluakoi Rd., at the old Kaluakoi Resort. Long, sandy beach, fronting on the Kaluakoi Hotel. Offers spectacular sunsets and views of the island of Oahu some 25 miles to the northwest. Good sunbathing possibilities; swimming not advised due to dangerous ocean conditions. No beach facilities.

Mo'omomi Beach. Located approximately 3½ miles northwest of Ho'olehua, bordering Mo'omomi Bay; reached by way of Farrington Ave., which turns into a rutted dirt road, to the very end. Long, undeveloped beach, frequented primarily by fishermen. Beachcombing possibilities; unsafe for swimming due to the prevailing ocean conditions and strong afternoon winds. No facilities.

Murphey's Beach Park. Off Kamehameha V Hwy. (450), 20 miles east of Kaunakakai. Sandy beach, protected by a reel just offshore, offering safe swimming conditions for children. Views of Moku Ho'oniki Island and Kanaha Rock to the northeast. No beach facilities.

Oneali'i Beach Park. Located 3 miles east of Kaunakakai, off Kamehameha V Hwy. (450). Narrow, sandy beach, with shallow water, ideal for swimming for children. Facilities include a pavilion, restrooms and ballpark. There is also an ancient fishpond at the beach.

Papohaku Beach. Situated just south of Kepuhi Beach, off Kaluakoi Rd., with at least three different access roads leading down to the beach. This is one of Hawaii's largest and most beautiful white-sand beaches, 3 miles long and, at places, nearly a hundred yards wide, bordered by kiawe trees. Views of Oahu; and showers and restroom facilities at one of the beach access points. Swimming not advised due to the strong under-currents.

MOLOKAI | Tours and Activities

Pohaku Mauliuli Beach (Make Horse Beach). North of Kepuhi Beach; reached by way of Kaka'ako Rd. (which goes off Kaluakoi Rd. at the Paniolo Hale Condominiums), then westward on Leo Place to the end. Picturesque crescent-shaped beach; unsafe for swimming due to the prevailing ocean conditions. No facilities.

Tours and Activities | Molokai

Father Damien Tours. Kalaupapa; (808) 567-6171. Offers hour-long guided van tours of the Kalaupapa Peninsula, with pick-up points at the bottom of the Pali trail and at the Kalaupapa Airport. Tours include all the points of interest on Kalaupapa, including the historic St. Philomena Church, built by Father Damien in 1872, and the Kalaupapa museum-cum-bookstore which has old, historic photos on display, as well as a good selection of books on Kalaupapa. Tour cost: $40.00 per person (must be 16 years of age or older). Advance reservations and permits required.

Fun Hogs Sportfishing. P.O. Box 424, Ho'olehua, HI 96729; (808) 567-6789/*www.molokaifishing.com*. Offers half-day and full-day deep-sea and near-shore sportfishing charters; also whale watches in season, and snorkeling and sightseeing tours and sunset cruises. Rates: $350.00-$450.00 for sportfishing trips; $65.00 per person for 2-hour whale watching or snorkeling tour.

Gypsy Sailing Adventures. Kaunakakai; (808) 558-8128/. Sailing charters around the island of Molokai on board a 33½-foot ocean-going catamaran, with private anchorages in coves and beaches accessible only by boat; also whale watching and inter-island cruising. Rates: $75.00 whale watching trip; $200.00-$500.00 for sailing excursions from 2 hours to full day.

Molokai Fish & Dive. P.O. Box 576. Kaunakakai, HI 96748; (808) 553-5926. Wide variety of tours, including scuba diving, sportfishing, whale watching; also mountain biking tours, horseback trail rides, and guided cultural hikes. Cost: $30.00-$85.00 for 2- to 6-hour guided hikes; $40.00-$85.00 for 4- to 6-hour mountain bike rides; $60.00-85.00 for 4- to 6-hour kayaking tours; $65.00 for 4-hour whale watches; $350.00-$500.00 for half- to full-day sportfishing excursions.

Molokai Mule Ride. P.O. Box 200 Kualapu'u, HI 96757; (808) 567-6088/(800) 567-7550/*www.muleride.com*. Mule Ride Tour (including entry permits for Kalaupapa National Park and a historical tour with Father Damien Tours): $165.00; Fly-In and Fly-Out Tour (from Molokai Airport to Kalaupapa, round trip, and historical tour with Father Damien Tours): $129.00. Also packages from Maui or Honolulu (with round trip air fare and mule ride) for $299.00

MOLOKAI | Tours and Activities

Molokai Charters. P.O. Box 1207, Kaunakakai, HI 96748; (808) 553-5852. Sailing charters of varying lengths, from 2 hours to half-day and full-day. The full-day trips include snorkeling and lunch at Lanai. Also whale-watching tours. Cost: $200.00-$500.00.

The Alyce C. (808) 558-8377. Sportfishing charters for deep sea fishing and trolling for marlin, spear fish, dorado, tuna. Also whale watching trips in season. 4-6 passenger limit. Rates range from $300.00 for half-day trips to $400.00 for full-day charters.

Golf Courses

Ironwood Hills Golf Club. Kualapu'u; (808) 567-6000. 9-hole, par-34 course, with good views of the island. Green fees: $18.00 for 9 holes, $23.00 for 18 holes; cart rental, $12.00. Club rentals available.

Kaluakoi Golf Course. At the Kaluakoi Resort, Kaluakoi Rd., Maunaloa; (808) 552-0255. 18-hole, par-72, oceanfront course. Green fees: $70.00 (including cart). Pro shop, driving range and putting green; also club rentals.

Events on the Island

January

Fourth Weekend. *Ka Molokai Makahiki Festival.* Held at the Kaunakakai Baseball Field in Kaunakakai. Ancient Hawaiian holiday, devoted to sports, games and celebration of life. Variety of music, food, and traditional Hawaiian games, including spear throwing and Hawaiian wrestling. For a schedule of events, call (808) 553-3673.

March

Fourth Weekend. *Prince Kuhio Day.* Celebration honoring Prince Kuhio, Hawaii's first delegate to the U.S. Congress; held in Kaunakakai. Features entertainment, and food concessions. For more information, call the Molokai Visitors Association at (808) 553-3876.

April

First Weekend. *Buddha Day.* Celebration of the birth of Buddha, with Buddhist festivities, including flower pageants, staged at Buddhist temples throughout the islands. For more information, call (808) 536-7044.

Third Weekend. *Earth Day Celebration.* Annual event, held at the Mitchell Pauole Center in Kaunakakai. Events and educational exhibits centered around the need for preservation of our natural and cultural resources. For more information, call The Nature Conservancy at (808) 553-5236.

May

Second Weekend. *Kaiwi Challenge Relay.* 39-mile race in one-man canoes across the Kaiwi Channel, between Molokai and Oahu. Begins at the old Kaluakoi Resort on Molokai's west shore and ends at the Outrigger Canoe Club in Waikiki, Oahu. More information at (808) 969-6695/www.kaikahoe.org.

Third Weekend. *Molokai Ka Hula Piko.* At the Papohaku Beach in Kaluakoi. Celebration of the birth of the hula, drawing a crowd of approximately 2,000 people. Features traditional Hawaiian arts and crafts, music, and local foods. For more information, call Destination Molokai at (808) 553-3876 or (800) 800-6367/www.molokaievents.com. *Starbuck's Kaiwi Channel Relay Race.* 32-mile kayak race, beginning at La'au Point on Molokai's west shore and ending at the Koko Marina, at Hawaii Kai, on the east shore of Oahu. Draws competitors from around the world. More information at (808) 222-5020/(808) 383-7798/www.y2kanu.com.

July

First Weekend. *4th of July.* Independence day parade held on the main street in Kaunakakai, and fireworks display at Oneali'i Beach Park, 3 miles cast of Kaunakakai. For more information, call the Molokai Visitors Association at (808) 553-6367/www.molokai-hawaii.com.

September

Fourth Weekend. *Bankoh Na Wahine o Ke Kai.* Women's 40.8-mile Molokai-to-Oahu outrigger canoe race, beginning at Hale o Lono Harbor in Molokai, and finishing at Duke Kahanamoku

Beach, Waikiki. For more information, call (808) 259-7112 or visit *www.holoholo.org. Molokai Music Festival.* Held at the Meyer Sugar Mill in Kalae. Features live music, presented by local Molokai performers; also hula dancing and demonstrations of traditional arts and crafts, and food concessions. For more information, call (808) 567-6436.

October

First Week. *Aloha Week.* Week-long festival, with events staged throughout the island. Features a variety of Hawaiian pageantry and demonstrations in lei making, poi pounding, coconut husking and coconut weaving. Also parades, arts and crafts, food, island fruit tasting, and entertainment—including original Hawaiian music and hula dancers. For a schedule of events, locations, and more information, call (808) 944-8857.

First Weekend. *Bankoh Molokai Hoe.* Men's 40.8-mile Molokai-to-Oahu outrigger canoe race, beginning at Hale o Lono Harbor in Molokai, and finishing at Fort DeRussy Beach in Waikiki. (808) 259-7112/*www.holoholo.org.*

December

First Weekend. *Bodhi Day.* Traditional Buddhist celebrations at temples throughout the islands, marking the Buddhist Day of Enlightenment. For more information, call (808) 536-7044.

Third Weekend. *Festival of Lights.* Electric Light Parade down Kaunakakai's main street, Ala Malama. Also island music and holiday arts and crafts. More information at (808) 553-3876/*www.molokai-hawaii.com.*

◀ ▮ UP 14 (◷)

= *Area Segment*

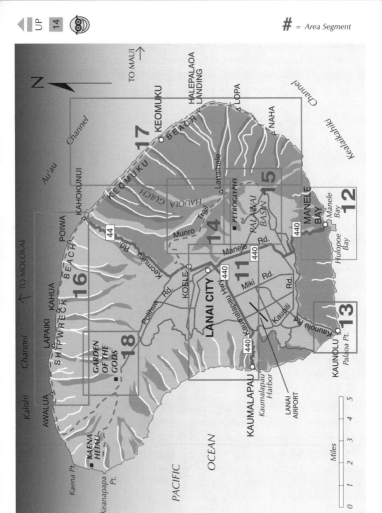

LANAI

Area segments, numerically coded, are described on the EXPLORING pages as indicated below:

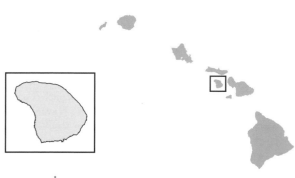

LANAI | The Private Isle

Lanai | Exploring the Island

Lanai is first and foremost a private island (which Bill Gates "rented" for his honeymoon in 1994—yes, the whole island!), owned in its entirety by a single entity, the Castle & Cooke Company. It is also a paradox, at once primitive and refined, where rugged, almost-inaccessible, four-wheel-drive country and the trappings of five-star, luxury resorts coexist.

The island is 18 miles long and 13 miles wide, all of 141 square miles, and unlike neighboring Maui and Molokai, it comprises a single volcanic land mass, that of Lanaihale, elevation 3,370 feet. At the center of the island is Lanai City, the island's chief community, and at its south end its principal resort, Manele Bay. To the southwest of Lanai City lies Kaunolu, to its east Keomuku Beach (a 6-mile coastal stretch), to its north an 8-mile stretch of coastline known as Shipwreck Beach, and to its northwest the eerie moonscape, Garden of the Gods. The Palawai Basin, once the largest pineapple plantation in the world, with 16,000-plus acres planted to the fruit at one time (fewer than 100 acres of pineapple now remain), lies just to the south of Lanai City.

For the purposes of exploring the island, we have divided Lanai into eight mini sections, since one each requires a separate trip, all radiating out from the island's hub, Lanai City:

Lanai City, where most of the island's population (approximately 3,100 in all) lives, and which includes the Lodge at Koele;

Manele Bay and Hulopoe Bay, which includes Manele Bay Hotel and a marine preserve along the south coast of the island;

Kaunolu, a village in the island's southwest corner;

Munro Trail, a historic and scenic trail east of Lanai City that traverses Lanaihale, the island's highest point;

Palawai Basin, the fertile, one-time pineapple-growing region;

Shipwreck Beach, a coastal strip along the north of the island;

East Coast, which takes in Keomuku Beach;

Garden of the Gods, the arid tract in the northwest part of the island.

LANAI | Lanai City

Lanai City

  See Map 15 for Orientation **11**

Lanai City is Lanai's principal population center, and its only town, situated more or less at the center of the island, to the north of Palawai Basin, at an elevation of 1,624 feet. It was originally built in the early 1920s as a plantation town by James Dole's Hawaii Pineapple Company which, in 1922, also purchased the island—yes, the entire island!—for a reported $1.1 million. The town is now home to a majority of the island's approximately 2,200 inhabitants. It is also quite picturesque, filled with the characteristic Norfolk Island pines and old, tin-roofed plantation-era houses, mostly set along a grid of a dozen or so paved streets.

2 Lanai City itself is one mile long and a half mile wide, and it has at the center of it the grassy, Norfolk Pine-lined **Dole Park**, with most of the local businesses—a shopping center, a market, two eateries, and a handful of shops—situated around the park, on Seventh, Eighth, Fraser and Lanai avenues. Here, too, at the southwest corner of Dole Park, is the town's jail, comprising three adjoining, free-standing cells, situated directly in front of the police station; and near the southeast end of the park, on Lanai Avenue, stands the

1 venerable old **Hotel Lanai**, originally built in the 1920s to accommodate James Dole's guests and visiting company executives. The hotel, for nearly seven decades, offered the only visitor accommodations on the island, with 10 guest rooms and a restaurant-cum-bar to boot. It remains quite popular with locals and visitors alike, most of them gathering here to exchange local gossip; and, needless to say, it continues to offer overnight lodging to guests.

3 One of the newest additions to Lanai City is the elegant **Lodge at Koele**, situated along Highway 44, just to the northeast of town, and nestled amid green meadows and towering pines and well-kept gardens overflowing with halaconias, orchids and torch ginger. The lodge opened to the public in 1991, and offers 102 well-appointed guest rooms, restaurants, swimming pool, tennis courts, lawn bowling, croquet facilities, and an 18-hole, Greg Norman and Ted Robinson-designed, championship golf course. The lodge also has a notable art collection of European and Pacific paintings and sculpture.

Also of interest, some 6 miles southwest of Lanai City, at the end of the Kaumalapau Highway (440), is the Kaumalapau Harbor, also built by the Dole interests to ship the company's pineapple to its canneries in Honolulu, and from where more than a million pineapples are still shipped daily. Here, too, as you approach the Kaumalapau Harbor, you can see, toward the north, five sea stacks, variously known as Nanahoa, Three Stones, and The Needles. The harbor is also a good place to enjoy Lanai's beautiful sunsets.

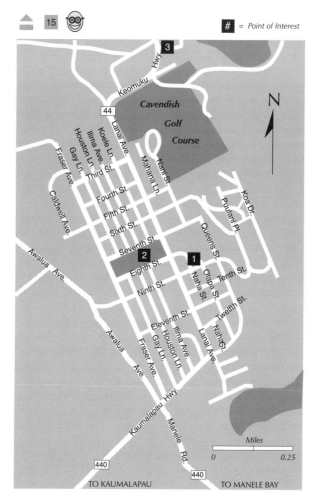

= Point of Interest

LANAI CITY

1. Hotel Lanai
2. Dole Park
3. The Lodge at Koele

LANAI | Manele Bay and Hulopoe Bay

Manele Bay and Hulopoe Bay | 12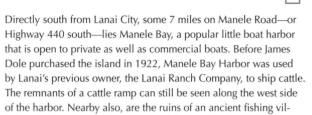

Directly south from Lanai City, some 7 miles on Manele Road—or Highway 440 south—lies Manele Bay, a popular little boat harbor that is open to private as well as commercial boats. Before James Dole purchased the island in 1922, Manele Bay Harbor was used by Lanai's previous owner, the Lanai Ranch Company, to ship cattle. The remnants of a cattle ramp can still be seen along the west side of the harbor. Nearby also, are the ruins of an ancient fishing village, with the foundations of some old Hawaiian houses still visible.

Also of interest, a little to the southwest of Manele Bay is Pu'u Pehe Cove, with a small, sandy beach, and just offshore from there rises a sea stack, the Pu'u Pehe Rock, also known as Sweetheart Rock, site of a tragic tale. Legend endures that Pu'u Pehe, a beautiful Maui woman, was kidnapped by a young warrior from Lanai, who, afraid that she would leave him, hid her in a sea cave here. But one day, while he was out fetching fresh water, a *kona* storm suddenly descended upon the area, sending huge waves of water gushing into the cave, trapping and killing the woman. Upon discovering the tragedy, the young warrior became distraught and carried Pu'u Pehe to the top of Sweetheart Rock, where he built a tomb for her; and soon after, he took his own life by jumping off the rock into the crashing sea below.

In any event, adjoining to the west of Pu'u Pehe Cove is Hulopoe Bay, at the head of which lies the crescent-shaped white-sand Hulopoe Beach, one of Hawaii's loveliest beaches. Hulopoe, besides having good swimming possibilities, offers some of the best snorkeling in the islands, with its abundant marine life and coral, all protected as part of the **Manele-Hulopoe Marine Life Conservatory District**. The beach also has picnic tables and barbecue pits, volleyball courts, and a nearby wading pool for children that was blasted from rock in 1951.

Directly above Hulopoe Beach, situated on a bluff overlooking both the beach and nearby Manele Bay, is the luxury **Manele Bay Hotel**, developed in 1991. The hotel offers 250 ocean view rooms, two plush restaurants—including one that features *koa* wood furnishings and decor in the traditional Hawaiian monarch style—a large swimming pool overlooking the beach, tennis courts, and an 18-hole golf course designed by Jack Nicklaus. The hotel also has splendid gardens—Japanese, Hawaiian and Filipino—and a collection of South Pacific art.

Kaunolu | 13

Kaunolu, situated at the southwest corner of the island, some 7 or 8 miles from Lanai City, is the site of an ancient fishing village which once also was the favorite vacation retreat of Kamehameha I and where you can still see the sites of some 86 houses and 35 shelters—one of the best preserved ruins in the Hawaiian islands. However, getting to Kaunolu can be an experience in itself, to say the least, journeying through pineapple fields and down rutted, dusty trails, largely unmarked. Nevertheless, for the stout of heart and limb, we suggest following Manele Road—Highway 440—south from Lanai City, nearly 4 miles, until the road makes a sharp left; and here, rather than following the highway to the left, continue straight ahead onto a dirt road—which has a sign pointing to Kaunolu, and which, incidentally, is Kaupili Road—that passes through pineapple fields. From the intersection of Kaupili Road and the highway (440), it is roughly 2½ miles to the fourth dirt road on the left which, by the way, is the Kaunolu Road—although you may not know this!—and which dashes off toward the ocean, another 3 miles or so, making a sharp left just three quarters of a mile from the turnoff and a sharp right a quarter mile farther, along an especially bumpy descent, to Kaunolu.

In any event, at the end of Kaunolu Road—which goes to the right at the three-way intersection, at the very bottom, at Kaunolu—you can search out the site of Kamehameha I's summer home, where you can still see the platform. Also, westward from here, across a gulch, you can see a large, domineering structure, the Halulu Heiau, reached by way of a short walk down the embankment and across the gulch to some stone walls on the opposite bank, from where a trail leads more or less directly to the *heiau*. There are also some petroglyphs here, depicting humans, birds and dancers, located just to the west of the *heiau*.

Westward from the Halulu Heiau and the petroglyphs, atop the sea cliffs, is the legendary Kahekili's Leap, a sheer, 90-foot drop to the crystal clear waters below, and from where, we are told, King Kamehameha I would force his warriors to jump, as a test of their courage and worthiness. Close to Kahekili's Leap, too, is Kolokolo Cave, in which you can hear the waves crashing and thundering; and just off shore from there is Moku Naio, or Shark Island, with its surprising resemblance to the fin of a shark. There are also good scuba diving and snorkeling possibilities here.

Finally, in Kaunolu itself you can search out ancient house sites, well over a hundred, mostly scattered through the Kaunolu Gulch. It is estimated that some 400 to 500 people may have once lived here.

The Munro Trail | 14

A highlight of any visit to Lanai is a drive—or hike—up the Munro Trail, an 8-mile trail just to the east of Lanai City, that winds through groves of Norfolk Island pine and a lush, tropical rain forest, journeying over the **Lanaihale** ridge—the highest point in Lanai, at an elevation of 3,370 feet. The trail is named for George C. Munro, an environmentalist and a native of New Zealand, who, while manager of the Lanai Ranch Company in the early 1900s, began planting seeds of the Norfolk Island Pine, indigenous to New Zealand, throughout the island to increase the island's water-drawing capacity. The Norfolk Pine, needless to say, is now characteristic of the island, abundant throughout Lanai City and along the Munro Trail.

In any case, the trailhead can be reached by following Keomuku Road—Highway 44—north from Lanai City, approximately 2 miles, then off on a paved road that goes off to the right—eastward—passing by a cemetery, another half mile or so, at which point it becomes a dirt trail—the Munro Trail. From here you can follow the signs for the Munro Trail, winding through groves of pine, eucalyptus and ironwood, as well as a lush, tropical rain forest, with spectacular views of Maunalei and Wahane gulches to the northeast.

Of interest, too, some 2½ miles along the trail, is the Ho'okio Battleground, site of a fierce battle between King Ka'akalaneo of the Big Island of Hawaii and the Lanaians. King Ka'akalaneo, it is told, after suffering losses and defeat at the hands of King Kahekili of Maui, turned his wrath on Lanai, and in the battle that ensued, Ka'akalaneo's heavily armed warriors drove the Lanaians from the Ho'okio Gulch up the Ho'okio Ridge, where they eventually weakened from lack of food and water, and were then slaughtered or driven over the ridge to their deaths. The site of the battleground can be identified by looking down toward the Ho'okio Ridge to the left of the trail—or northward—and locating at the crest of the ridge three successive indentations, which in reality are 20-foot wide, 8-foot-deep trenches, dug out and used by the Lanaians as their last defense.

Farther still, another mile or so, is the 3,370-foot summit of Lanaihale, the highest peak on Lanai, from where you can see, on clear days, nearly all the inhabited islands of Hawaii—Oahu, Molokai, Maui, Kaho'olawe and the Big Island. Also from Lanaihale you can view the 2,000-foot-deep Hauola Gulch, Lanai's deepest canyon, as it winds toward the ocean.

The Munro Trail finally descends into the Palawai Basin, from where you can journey northwestward on the Hoike Road, an unmarked dirt trail that eventually merges with Manele Road—Highway 440—one and one-half miles south of Lanai City.

LANAI | Palawai Basin

Palawai Basin | 15

The Palawai Basin, encompassing some 6 square miles and lying just to the south of Lanai City, is essentially the crater of an extinct volcano that originally formed the island of Lanai. Interestingly, it was once also the site of a Mormon colony, appropriately named the "City of Joseph," established in 1854. The colony, however, failed in 1857, but was attempted again, a few years later, in 1861, under the leadership of a particularly enterprising Mormon missionary named Walter Murray Gibson. Gibson, as it turned out, was a man on a mission of his own. In the years following the establishment of the colony, he purchased large tracts of land, supposedly for the Mormon Church, but systematically registering all the titles in his name; until, by 1875, he controlled fully 90% of all the land on Lanai, devoting much of it to goat and sheep ranching. Needless to say, the Mormon Church excommunicated Mr. Gibson forthwith, and the Mormon colony failed for the last time.

At any rate, Palawai Basin's chief interest lies in the Luahiwa Petroglyphs—quite possibly the best preserved petroglyphs in the islands—reached by way of Manele Road—Highway 440—south from Lanai City, one and one-half miles, then left—or southeast—on Hoike Road, an unmarked dirt road that journeys through pineapple fields. From Hoike Road, a mile or so from the Manele Road turnoff, a dirt trailheads off northward roughly three quarters of a mile to the petroglyphs, which can be found on several boulders scattered on a hillside beneath some trees. The **Luahiwa Petroglyphs** feature symbols and stick figures representing humans, animals and birds, quite possibly dating from the late 1700s or early 1800s. The practice of making petroglyphs, of course, dates from the time of the first arrivals in Hawaii, and consists of etchings or carvings on rocks, made by either a blunt or sharp, pointed tool; they feature symbols and stick figures of humans and animals—frequently thought to represent supernatural beings or gods—depicting scenes from daily life, such as hunting or dancing scenes. It is believed that much of the activity surrounding these petroglyphs occurred just before the arrival of Captain Cook in the islands in 1778, and continued until the 1860s.

Shipwreck Beach | 16

Shipwreck Beach is the name given to the 8-mile stretch of coastline along the island's remote north coast, just offshore from where, on the reef in the Kalohi Channel, several ships have run aground over the years—hence the notoriety and the name. Shipwreck

Beach itself comprises four or five smaller beaches—Awalua, Lapaiki, Po'aiwa, Federation Camp—all quite secluded, and with narrow strips of sand, backed by shallow sand dunes. The beaches offer some beachcombing and shoreline fishing possibilities, but swimming and snorkeling are not encouraged here due to the choppy seas.

In any case, Shipwreck Beach can be reached by way of Keomuku Road—Highway 430—north from Lanai City, some 6½ miles to the very bottom, where the paved road finally ends; then west on a rugged coastal road, a mile or so, to Federation Camp—a beach area used primarily by members of the Filipino Federation of America, a religious, cultural and social organization—and Po'aiwa, the last relatively easily accessible point on Shipwreck Beach. At **Po'aiwa** you can search out the ruins of an old lighthouse, just to the north of the parking area, and also see a shipwreck just offshore from there—one of only two visible along the coast here—believed to be that of a concrete-mud barge, run aground in 1960. Also from here, a marked trail following painted rocks leads inland a little way to some well-preserved petroglyphs depicting human figures, dogs, centipedes, and hunting scenes.

Westward from Po'aiwa, of course, lie Lapaiki and Awalua, 5 miles and 7 miles, respectively, reached on a wild sort of coastal trail, accessible, for the most part, on foot. Both beaches offer some fishing possibilities, but little else; and from Awalua you can see the second of the two visible shipwrecks along the coast here, reportedly that of an old oil tanker, dating from the 1950s. Alawua and Lapaiki can also be reached by way of steep, rugged trails leading down from Polihua Road—which leads northwestward from Lanai City to the Garden of the Gods.

Lanai's East Coast | 17

The east coast of Lanai is comprised primarily of Keomuku Beach—a 6-mile coastal stretch extending from Kahokunui southeast to Halepalaoa—and south from Keomuku Beach to Lopa and Naha, two ancient fishing villages. The east coast of Lanai, specifically the site of Lae Hi—unmarked, and difficult to locate—also has associations with Prince Kaulula'au, son of Maui's King Ka'akalaneo. According to local lore, in the 1400s, Kaulula'au was banished to Lanai—an island inhabited solely by evil spirits at the time—as punishment for his incessant, mischievous behavior. As the story goes, the young prince was left ashore on Lanai's east coast near the site of Lae Hi, and, mischievous as he was, he eluded the island's evil spirits by sleeping in a secret cave by the sea at night while the spirits searched for him in vain. The spirits finally concluded that he was sleeping in the surf in the ocean, and when they eventually looked for him there, they drowned. Thus were the evil spirits of Lanai vanquished from the island, making it safe for habitation by humans, and Prince Kaulula'au, as one would expect, returned to Maui a hero.

In any case, **Keomuku Beach**, quite like the adjacent Shipwreck Beach, can be reached more or less directly on Keomuku Road—Highway 430—some 6½ miles north from Lanai City. At the north end of Keomuku Road (where the paved portion of the road ends), near the head of Keomuku Beach, sits Kahokunui; and roughly 5½ miles southeast from there, along a wild and bumpy dirt road that journeys along the coast, lies Keomuku, site of the failed Maunalei sugar plantation. It was here, in 1898, that Walter Gibson's daughter, Talula, and her husband, Frederick Hayselden, attempted to establish a sugar plantation, forming the Maunalei Sugar Company. A pier was constructed at Halepalaoa Landing, just south of Keomuku, and during the process of building a railroad from Keomuku to Halepalaoa, in order to obtain stones for laying the tracks, the company blasted part of the nearby Kahe'a Heiau—which can still be seen in its dismantled state, just inland from Keomuku Road, a mile or so south of Keomuku. According to popular belief, it was this act of desecrating a sacred *heiau* that signaled the beginning of the end of the Maunalei company. In a matter of days, following the partial destruction of the *heiau*, the water for the mill turned brackish at its very source and the plantation failed not long after, in 1900, when the company's Japanese labor force died of the plague that swept through the islands that year. Remnants of an old, abandoned locomotive can still be seen here, just inland from the main road, a little over a mile and a half south of Keomuku, reached by way of a short walk; and a little farther to the south, situated alongside the road itself, is a Japanese cemetery where the Japanese laborers from the Maunalei company, who died of the plague, are buried.

At Keomuku itself, you can see some sites of the plantation town's homes, now overgrown with weeds. Here, too, amid a grove of coconut palms, is the old, ramshackle **Ka Lanakila O Ka Malamalama Church**, the last structure to be left standing in Keomuku. The church dates from 1903, and is claimed to be the oldest church on the island. Also worth investigating, just to the north and south of Keomuku, respectively, on the *makai*—ocean—side of the road, are the ruins of the ancient Ka'a and Wai'opae fishponds, both visible at low tide.

Farther still, some 4 miles south of Keomuku—2 miles south of Halepalaoa and the Japanese cemetery—lies **Lopa**, which has a small, sandy beach, with one or two picnic tables. Lopa also has in it an ancient fishpond, the remnants of which can be seen just to the south of the beach, beneath some palms.

Another 3 miles south from Lopa and we are at Naha, where the Keomuku Road finally ends. Naha is a former fishing village that is still frequented primarily by fishermen. It has, nevertheless, a fish-pond of interest, as well as an ancient paved trail, accessed only on foot, that leads from Naha to the Palawai Basin. The trailhead lies just to the south of the end of Keomuku Road, reached by crossing over a dry river bed and following a shoreline trail a short distance to the old paved trail that dashes off inland. There are also some good views, a little way along the trail from the trailhead, of the islands of Maui and Kaho'olawe.

Garden of the Gods | 18

The "Garden of the Gods," many will tell you, is one of Lanai's hidden gems, especially interesting to geology buffs. It is located in the remote, rugged northern part of the island, and reached by way of Fraser Street directly northwest from Lanai City, passing through pineapple fields just on the outskirts of town, then Polihua Road—a dirt road—also northwestward, nearly 6 miles, to the unusual, eerie landscape of the Garden of the Gods.

▶ The **Garden of the Gods** is indeed a strange, natural phenomenon where, in an eroded canyon of red soil, scores of boulders of varying shapes, sizes and colors—in hues of red, blue and orange—lie scattered about, creating a moonscape of sorts. At sunset, the colors in the landscape are especially stunning, and well worth photographing. There are also good views of the ocean from here.

From the Garden of the Gods, too, for the hardy souls, a rugged trail leads down to the remote, secluded Polihua Beach, some 4½ miles distant, with the last half mile or so accessible only on foot. Polihua—meaning "eggs in the bosom," and named for the fact that it was once a favorite nesting place for green sea turtles—is a beautiful, white-sand beach, rarely visited, and with great views of Molokai across the Kalohi Channel. It is, however, also rather windy and unsafe for swimming due to the strong ocean currents.

▶ Finally, there is the **Ka'ena Heiau**, the largest *heiau* on the island, approximately 55 feet wide and 150 feet long, situated on a bluff overlooking the ocean, some 4 or 5 miles northwest of the Garden of the Gods. The *heiau* can be reached by way of the Polihua Trail, a mile from the Garden of the Gods, then the Ka'ena Trail that branches to the left, off the Polihua Trail, with the last 3 miles or so virtually impassable, leaving it only to the sure-footed and iron-willed to make the pilgrimage.

In any event, from the Garden of the Gods you must retrace your steps, on Polihua Road, back to Lanai City.

Accommodations

Hotel Lanai. *$105-$175*. 828 Lanai Ave., Lanai City; (808) 565-7211/(800) 795-7211/*www.hotellanai.com*. 10 units. Restaurant and cocktail lounge on premises.

The Lodge at Koele. *$400-$2,200*. Keomuku Hwy. (44), Lanai City; (808) 565-7300/(800) 321-4666/*www.islandoflanai.com*. 102-unit luxury hotel. Room phones, swimming pool, tennis court, golf course, stables, restaurants and cocktail lounge, and meeting rooms.

The Manele Bay Hotel. *$400-$3,500*. Manele Bay Rd. (440), Manele Bay; (808) 565-7700/(800) 321-4666/*www.islandoflanai. com*. 250 rooms and suites in oceanfront resort hotel. Room phones and air-conditioning; also swimming pool, health club and spa, golf course, tennis courts, restaurants and cocktail lounge, meeting rooms, and beauty salon.

Dining

[Restaurant prices—based on full-course dinner, excluding drinks, tax and tips—are categorized as follows: *Deluxe*, over $30; *Expensive*, $20-$30; *Moderate*, $10-$20. *Inexpensive*, under $10.]

Blue Ginger Cafe. *Inexpensive-Moderate*. 409 7th Ave., Lanai City; (808) 565 6363. Local island fare, including burgers, salads, stir-fry and Japanese and Chinese preparations; also plate lunches, and freshly-baked pastries for breakfast. Open Sun.-Thurs. 6 a.m.-8 p.m., Fri.-Sat. 6 a.m.-9 p.m.

Café 565. *Inexpensive-Moderate*. 408 8th St., Lanai City; (808) 565-6622. Casual setting. Offers home-style plate lunches, sandwiches, salads and desserts; also thin-crust pizzas, calzone and noodles. Open for lunch and dinner.

Canoes Lanai. Inexpensive-Moderate. 419 7th Ave., Lanai City; (808) 565-6537. Popular local eatery. Offers home-style breakfast, plate lunches, and burgers. Open for breakfast and lunch daily (except Wed.).

Hotel Lanai. Inexpensive-Moderate. 828 Lanai Ave., Lanai City; (808) 565-7211. Serves hearty breakfasts, and lunches and dinners featuring fresh fish, pasta, steaks and poultry; also salad bar. Open for breakfast, lunch and dinner daily.

Hulopoe Court. Moderate-Expensive. At the Manele Bay Hotel, Manele Rd. (Hwy. 440), Manele Bay; (808) 565-7700. Casual, ocean view restaurant. Features contemporary Hawaiian regional cuisine, served in a Mediterranean setting. Open for breakfast and dinner daily. Reservations suggested.

Ihilani. Expensive-Deluxe. At the Manele Bay Hotel, Manele Rd. (Hwy. 440), Manele Bay; (808) 565-7700. Well-appointed restaurant in open-air setting, overlooking Hulopoe Bay. Serves gourmet French-Mediterranean cuisine. Open for dinner, 6 p.m.-9.30 p.m. Tues.-Sat. Reservations required.

The Lodge at Koele. Deluxe. At The Lodge at Koele, Keomuku Rd. (Hwy. 44), Lanai City; (808) 565-7300. Formal dining room in elegant setting, offering contemporary New American cuisine. Menu features fresh fish, lobster, steak, and axis deer. Open for dinner, 6 p.m.-9.30 p.m. daily. Reservations recommended; jackets required for men.

Pele's Other Garden. *Moderate.* Lanai City; (808) 565-9628. New York-style deli -cum-bistro, serving primarily salads, sandwiches, burritos, soups, pizzas and pasta dishes, and desserts. Take-outs available. Open for lunch and dinner.

The Pool Grille. Moderate. Manele Bay Hotel, Manele Rd., Manele Bay; (808) 565-7700. Casual pool side restaurant, serving primarily sandwiches, salads, burgers and grilled entrees. Also cocktails. Open 11 a.m.-5 p.m. daily.

The Terrace. *Expensive.* At the Lodge at Koele, Keomuku Rd. (44), Lanai City; (808) 565-7300. Casual setting; overlooking beautiful gardens and a reflection pond. Offers contemporary Hawaiian cuisine, with emphasis on fresh fish, steak and lobster. Breakfast, lunch and dinner daily. Reservations suggested.

THINGS TO SEE AND DO

Places to See | Points of Interest at a Glance

Garden of the Gods. Located in the remote, rugged northern part of the island, and reached by way of Fraser St. northwest from Lanai City to the outskirts of town, then Polihua Rd., a dirt road, another 6 miles northwestward to the Garden of the Gods. This is one of the island's foremost attractions where, in an eroded canyon of red soil, scores of boulders of various shapes, sizes and colors—in hues of red, blue and orange, especially vibrant at sunset—lie scattered about, creating a lunar landscape of sorts. There are also good views of the ocean from here.

Hulopoe Beach. At the bottom end of Hwy. 440 (Manele Rd.), approximately 7 miles south of Lanai City. Crescent-shaped white-sand beach, one of Hawaii's loveliest beaches, situated at the head of Hulopoe Bay. Offers some of the best snorkeling and diving in the islands, with abundant marine life and coral, all protected as part of the Manele-Hulopoe Marine Life Conservatory District. Also safe swimming conditions, including a nearby natural rock wading pool for children, and picnic tables, barbecue pits, and volleyball courts.

Kaunolu. Located in the southwest corner of the island, nearly 8 miles from Lanai City, and reached by way of Manele Rd. (440) south from Lanai City some 4 miles, then westward onto Kaupili Rd., a rugged dirt road, another 2½ miles, from where the wild Kaunolu Rd. dashes off toward the ocean, another 3 miles or so—making a sharp left just three-quarter mile from the Kaupili Rd. turnoff and a sharp right a quarter mile farther—along an especially bumpy descent, to Kaunolu. Kaunolu itself is the site of an ancient fishing village, which was once the favorite vacation retreat of Kamehameha I and which still has in it the sites of some 86 houses and 35 shelters—one of the best preserved ruins in the Hawaiian islands. There is also a large *heiau* here, the Halulu Heiau, together with some petroglyphs, and Kahekili's Leap, with its sheer, 90-foot drop to the ocean below.

The Luahiwa Petroglyphs. Located in the Palawai Basin, more or less in the center of the island; reached by way of Manele Rd. (440) south from Lanai City, approximately 1½ miles (just past mile marker 7), then left—southeast—on Hoike Rd., an unmarked dirt road, another mile or so, and off on a dirt trail (which goes off Hoike Rd.), northward, roughly three quarters of a mile, to the petroglyphs. The Luahiwa Petroglyphs are among the best preserved petroglyphs in the islands, quite possibly dating from the late 1700s and early 1800s, and featuring symbols and stick figures representing humans, animals and birds.

Munro Trail. 8-mile trail, just to the east of Lanai City. The trailhead is located northeast of Lanai City, a mile past the Lodge at Koele, with the sign-posted trailheading off eastward from Keomuku Rd. (Hwy. 44), winding through groves of Norfolk Island pine and a lush, tropical rain forest, passing over the Lanaihale ridge, the highest point in Lanai, at an elevation of 3,370 feet, with views of the 2,000-foot-deep Hauola Gulch, the Maunalei and Wahane gulches, and, on clear days, the islands of Oahu, Molokai, Maui, Kaho'olawe and Hawaii. The trail is accessible only in a four-wheel-drive vehicle, or on foot.

Shipwreck Beach. Situated along the island's remote north coast, and reached on Keomuku Rd. (Hwy. 430) north from Lanai City, some 6½ miles, to the very end, then west on a rugged, coastal dirt road, another mile or so, to the start of the beach. The beach comprises approximately 8 miles of shoreline, including a series of smaller beach areas—Federation Camp, Po'aiwa, Lapaiki and Awalua—all quite secluded, and with narrow strips of sand, backed by shallow sand dunes. The beaches offer some beach-combing and shoreline fishing possibilities, but swimming and snorkeling are not encouraged due to the choppy seas. There are also two shipwrecks visible just offshore from the beach—one of a concrete-mud barge run aground in 1960, and another of an old oil tanker, dating from the 1950s.

Keomuku. Situated on the east coast of the island, east of Lanai City, and reached by way of Keomuku Rd. (Hwy. 430) north from Lanai City, 6½ miles, to the very end, then southeast along the coast another 5½ miles on a bumpy dirt road to Keomuku. Keomuku itself is the site of the failed, late 19th-century Maunalei sugar plantation, where the sites of some old plantation homes are still visible, as well as the old ramshackle Ka Lanakila O Ka Malamalama Church, the last structure to be left standing in Keomuku, dating from 1903 and with the distinction of being the oldest church on the island, nestled in a grove of coconut palms.

Tours and Activities

Golf Courses

The Experience at Koele. Keomuku Rd. (44), Lanai City; (808) 565-4653. 18-hole, championship course, at an elevation of 1,600 feet, designed by Greg Norman; 7,102 yards, par 72. Green fees: $95.00-$140.00 (including cart). Pro shop, driving range, and club rentals.

The Challenge at Manele Bay. Manele Bay; (808) 565-3800. 18-hole, Jack Nicklaus-designed championship course; 7,000-7,600 yards, par 72. Green fees: $99.00 for guests of Manele Bay Hotel, $140.00 for non-guests. Pro shop, driving range, club rentals.

Tennis

The Lodge at Koele. Keomuku Rd. (Hwy. 44), Lanai City, (808) 565-7300. The resort has 3 courts with no lights. Open to the public. Available to hotels guests at no cost, and to non-guest for a fee of around $20.00 per person, per day.

Manele Bay Hotel. Manele Bay Rd. (440), Manele Bay, (808) 565-7700/(800) 321-4666. Offer 6 courts, also with no lights. Open to the public; available to hotel guests at no cost, and to non-guests for around $20.00 per day.

HAWAIIAN GLOSSARY

The Hawaiian language, in its simplicity, contains only seven consonants—H, K, L, M, N, P, W—and five vowels—A, E, I, O and U. All words—and syllables—end in a vowel, and all syllables begin with a consonant. The vowels, typically, are each pronounced separately—i.e., a'a is pronounced "ah-ah," and e'e is pronounced "ay-ay"; the only exceptions are the diphthong double vowels—ai, pronounced "eye," and *au,* pronounced "ow." The consonants, on the other hand, are never doubled.

Hawaiian consonants are pronounced similar to those in English, with the notable exception of W, which is sometimes pronounced as "V," when it begins the last syllable of the word. Hawaiian vowels are pronounced as follows: A- "uh," as in among; E - "ay," as in day; I - "ee," as in deep; O - "oh," as in no; U - "oo," as in blue.

For travellers to the Hawaiian islands, the following is a glossary of some commonly used words in the Hawaiian language.

a'a — rough, crumbling lava.

ae — yes.

ahi — tuna fish.

ahupua'a — pie-shaped land division, extending from the mountains to the sea.

aikane — friend.

alanui — road, or path.

ali'i — a Hawaiian chief or nobleman.

aloha — love, or affection; traditional Hawaiian greeting, meaning both welcome and farewell.

anu — cold, cool.

a'ole — no.

auwe — alas!

awawa — valley.

hala — the pandanus tree, the leaves of which are used to make baskets and mats.

hale — house.

hale pule — church; house of worship.

hana — work.

hahana — hot, warm.

haole — foreigner; frequently used to refer to a Caucasian.

hapa — half, as in *hapa-haole,* or half Caucasian.

haupia — coconut cream pudding, often served at a *luau.*

heiau — an ancient Hawaiian place of worship; shrine, temple.

holoholo — to go for a walk; also to ride or sail.

honi — a kiss; also, to kiss.

hui — a group, society, or assembly of people.

hukilau — a communal fishing party, in which everyone helpspull in the fishing nets.

hula — traditional Hawaiian dance of storytelling.

imu — underground oven, used for roasting pigs for *luaus.*

ipo — sweetheart, or lover.

ka'ahele — a tour.

ka'ao — legend.

kahuna — priest, minister, sorcerer, prophet.

kai — the sea.

kakahiaka — morning.

kama'aina — native-born, or local.

kanaka — man, usually of Hawaiian descent.

kane — male, husband.

kapu —taboo, forbidden; derived from the Tongan word, *tabu.*

keiki — child; a male child is known as *keikikane,* and a female child, *keikiwahine.*

kiawe — Algaroba tree, with fern-like leaves and sharp, long thorns, usually found in dry areas near the coast. Kiawe wood is used to make charcoal for fuel. The tree was introduced to Hawaii in the 1820s.

koa — native Hawaiian tree, prized for its wood which was used by early Hawaiians to craft canoes, spears and surf-boards. Koa wood is now used to make fine furniture.

kokua — help.

kona — leeward side of island; frequently used to describe storms and winds, such as *kona* storm or *kona* wind. Also, south.

ko'olau — windward side of island.

kukui — Candlenut tree, characteristic in its yellow and green foliage, generally found in the valleys. Kukui nuts are also used in *leis.* Kukui is Hawaii's state tree.

kuleana — home site, or homestead; also responsibility, or one's business.

kupuna — grandparent.

lamalama — torch fishing

lanai — porch, veranda, balcony.

lani — the sky, or heaven

laulau — wrapped package; generally used to describe bundles of pork, fish or beef, served with *taro* shoots, wrapped in *ti* or banana leaves, and steamed.

lei — garland, wreath, or necklace of flowers.

lilikoi — passion fruit.

limu — seaweed.

luau — traditional Hawaiian feast.

mahalo — thanks, or thank you.

mahi-mahi — dolphin.

maile — native vine with shiny, fragrant leaves used in leis.

makahiki hou — New Year; *hauoli makahiki hou,* Happy New

Year.

make — to die, or dead.

makai — toward the ocean, or seaward.

malihini — stranger, newcomer.

mana — supernatural power.

manu — bird.

mauka — toward the mountain, or inland.

mauna — mountain.

mele — song, chant.

menehune — Hawaii's legendary little people, ingenious and hardworking, who worked only at night, building fishponds, heiaus, irrigation ditches and roads, many of which remain today.

moana — the ocean; open sea.

mo'o — lizard, dragon, serpent.

mu'umu'u — long, loose, traditional Hawaiian dress.

nani — beautiful.

nui — big.

ohana — family.

ono — delicious.

pakalolo — marijuana.

palapala — book; also printing.

pali — cliff; also plural, cliffs.

paniolo — Hawaiian cowboy.

pau — finished, all done.

poi — a purplish paste made from pounded and cooked *taro* roots; staple of Hawaiian diet.

GLOSSARY | Hawaiian Words

puka — hole, opening.

pupu — appetizer, snack, hors d'oeuvre.

pupule — crazy; insane.

tapa — cloth made from beaten bark, often used in Hawaiian clothing.

taro — broad-leafed plant with starch root, used to make poi; staff of life of early Hawaiians, introduced to the islands by the first Polynesians.

ti — broad-leafed plant, brought to Hawaii by early Polynesian immigrants. *Ti* leaves are used for wrapping food as well as offerings to the gods.

waha — mouth; *waha nui, a* big mouth.

wahine — female, woman, wife.

wai — fresh water.

wiki — to hurry; *wikiwiki,* hurry up.

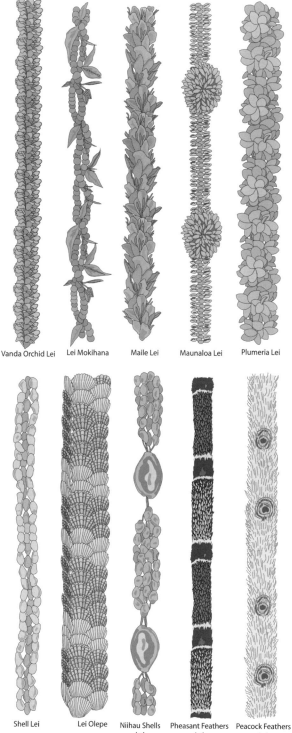

Vanda Orchid Lei   Lei Mokihana   Maile Lei   Maunaloa Lei   Plumeria Lei

Shell Lei   Lei Olepe   Niihau Shells Lei   Pheasant Feathers Lei   Peacock Feathers Lei

INDEX